W9-CNW-831

CHURCH
BUDGET
DEVELOPMENT

Harry Robert Page

PRENTICE-HALL, INC.
Englewood Cliffs, New Jersey

PRENTICE-HALL INTERNATIONAL, INC., *London*
PRENTICE-HALL OF AUSTRALIA, PTY., LTD., *Sydney*
PRENTICE-HALL OF CANADA, LTD., *Toronto*
PRENTICE-HALL OF INDIA (PRIVATE) LTD., *New Delhi*
PRENTICE-HALL OF JAPAN, INC., *Tokyo*
PRENTICE-HALL DE MEXICO, S.A., *Mexico City*

CHURCH BUSINESS MANAGEMENT SERIES

VOLUMES PUBLISHED

Church Budget Development, Harry R. Page
Church Accounting Methods, Arthur L. Walker
Church Fund Raising, George W. Harrison
Managing Church Business Through Group Procedures, Robert
   R. Powell
Personal Finance for Clergymen, John C. Bramer, Jr.
Church Purchasing Procedures, Julian Feldman

VOLUMES IN PREPARATION

Insurance for the Church, John C. Bramer, Jr.
Church Public Relations, Ole S. Johnson
Acquiring and Developing Church Real Estate, Joseph Stiles
Maintaining and Using Church Property, Allen W. Graves
Church Office Management, Arthur L. Walker
Your Church Secretary, Allen W. Graves

EDITOR'S INTRODUCTION

THE SERIES of books in which this volume is included was prepared for all who seek new insight and specific guidance in administering business affairs of churches. These books represent the most comprehensive publishing project ever completed in the field of church business management.

Each book in the series is based on two major premises: First, if churches are to accomplish their purposes effectively, their business affairs must be managed as well as, or better than, those of other organizations. Second, since churches are service-rendering rather than profit-making, and because of their voluntary nature and the trustee relationship involved, their business policies and practices must differ in certain respects from those of commercial enterprises and the differences must be clearly identified and thoroughly understood.

These books are intended (1) to help clergy and laity develop additional competence for effective stewardship of church business responsibilities, (2) to provide stimulation and practical suggestions for professional career employment as business managers of churches and related non-profit organizations, and (3) to make available an educational basis for strengthening the role of pastors as chief administrators of individual churches.

In planning, organizing, and evaluating this series of books the editor was confronted with certain basic questions to which explicit answers had not been published. What *is* church business management? What is it *for?* What is it *not?* What is it *not for?* What are its boundaries? The following tentative definition by the editor is the result of his pioneer effort to delineate and identify this field:

Church Business Management is the science and art of administering church program development, financial resources, physical facilities, office services, staff personnel, and public relations, all in accordance with the most effective standards of religious stewardship. Included in this concept are such managerial processes as forecasting, planning, organizing, delegating, controlling, evaluating, and reporting. Management of a church's business responsibilities is a facilitating function to be regarded not as an end in itself but as an important means to a worthy end.

Illustrations of what may be considered "church business management" have come from congregations that have added a professional business manager to the employed staff. A carefully written job description for such a staff member usually can help any church identify the business functions that are essential in establishing and attaining its distinctive purposes. Such job descriptions should, and often do, represent the business manager as a professional consultant and resource leader in helping church officers and staff, both volunteers and employees, perform their administrative duties in relation to the ministry of:

1. *Program Development*—planning, organizing, and scheduling all appropriate means available to the church for achieving its objectives and goals.
2. *Financial Management*—budgeting, obtaining, safeguarding, disbursing, and accounting for all financial resources.
3. *Property Management*—using, maintaining, and acquiring

physical facilities such as buildings and grounds, furniture, and equipment.

4. *Office Management*—providing systematic programs of scheduling, communicating, and recording services to facilitate achievement of administrative functions.

5. *Personnel Management*—determining and describing staff positions; enlisting, assigning, and training nonprofessional staff, both volunteers and employees; developing and maintaining staff morale.

6. *Public Relations*—communicating the church's concept of its purposes, its programs, its accomplishments, its potentialities, and its needs.

Church business management as viewed in this light, and when applied creatively through proper use of collaborative and democratic procedures, is a significant phase of a meaningful spiritual ministry. How successfully and effectively the author of each book in this series has amplified the foregoing philosophy and specifications each reader will, of course, judge for himself.

For invaluable advice and practical assistance on various phases of this endeavor the editor is grateful to Dr. Nathan A. Baily, Dean of the School of Business Administration, The American University. Dean Baily's keen interest in this field and his able leadership in establishing the American University Center for Church Business Management were significant factors in the development of this series of books.

Clyde W. Humphrey
General Editor

Washington, D. C.

PREFACE

THIS BOOK has as its objective increased effectiveness in planning and controlling the financial resources of the individual church. Budget development and use are treated here as an administrative process common to churches of all denominations and sizes.

This volume describes the underlying purposes of budgeting, its advantages and limitations, and its relationship to current activities, programs, and future plans of the church. The budgetary process is developed in detail, including the sequence of actions leading to approval and implementation, the responsibilities to be shared, and the participation necessary. Various techniques and devices useful in church budgeting are explored, individual treatment being given many items of church income and expense.

Much of this material was assembled in connection with two sessions of the Institute on Church Finance conducted in 1962 by the Center for Church Business Management, a unit of The American University School of Business Administration, working in cooperation with Wesley Theological Seminary. Representatives of thirteen religious denominations and forty-eight individual churches across the country participated in week-long seminars on church budget development. Many of the illustrations and examples were contributed by that group. Other examples were furnished by stewardship councils and committees, as is indicated on the individual exhibits. Appreciation is expressed to all who assisted in this manner. I also wish to thank Marie Olsson and Dorothy Couture for their excellent work in preparing the manuscript.

Harry Robert Page

Washington, D.C.

CONTENTS

9

LIST OF EXHIBITS

Part I

The Concept and Philosophy
of Church Budgeting

Chapter 1

PROGRAMS AND BUDGETS

EVERY CHURCH OR SYNAGOGUE is both a spiritual and a social group. Each is also an economic unit, with the recurring economic problems of demand and supply.

This book is concerned with financial and material demands, and with efforts to meet those demands in the spirit of religious stewardship. Its central objective is that of increasing the effectiveness of planning and controlling the financial resources of churches. Such effectiveness will come about through greater understanding of budgeting as an administrative process. Knowledge of concepts and methods used successfully in business and government form part of this understanding.

This book does three things:

It establishes a frame of reference in which the church budget can really be understood and appreciated. This is done in Part I, The Concept and Philosophy of Church Budgeting.

It explains and illustrates the budgetary documents normally developed, and treats in detail many components of church expense and revenue. This is done in Part II, The Church Budget in Preparation.

It shows how the budget is used in connection with planning, coordinating and controlling the business affairs of churches. This is done in Part III, The Church Budget in Use.

The intention here is to provide not only a practical guide or handbook for use in developing church budgets, but also to establish and amplify the concept of budgeting as the "hub" of church business management.

This book is directed to those responsible for the sustained effectiveness of churches, as that effectiveness is influenced by material support. Specifically, it is written for both ministers and lay leaders; including but not limited to finance board chairmen, program and budget committee chairmen, treasurers, business managers, administrators, and secretaries.

To facilitate the use of this book in studying and teaching church business administration, the discussion outline for Church Budget Development as used at the American University Center for Church Business Management, has been included. It will be found as Appendix A, beginning on page 173.

THE OBJECTIVE OF THE BUDGET

Extensive material resources are needed to achieve the full mission and role of local churches. Good budget procedure is essential to effective acquisition and application of these resources. The budget is a church's plan and commitment to support its stated objectives and programs.

To realize the full benefits of good budgeting, we must appreciate the true place of the budget in the life of the church. The budget is a reflection of the goals and objectives of the church, and a description of how they are to be met. It is a commitment and authorization to carry out or to attain established goals and objectives. Success in budgeting should be judged not by how precisely the budget document was prepared and how closely the financial situation was forecast, but by how nearly the church's objectives and programs were met—or perhaps by how far they were exceeded.

The budget is a means to an end. The program comes first, and should control the budget—not the other way around. This means that the plans and programs of the church have been subject to prior deliberation, and that budgeting becomes a "costing out" of matters previously considered.

Specifically then, the budget is a twofold tabulation of the dollar expenditures considered necessary in accomplishing the work of the church, and the anticipated income or revenue from which those expenditures will be met. It is thus a forecast and a plan, stated in dollars and dates. As we shall see, this forecast and accompanying plan has several parts, several versions, and several phases.

SOUND AND IMAGINATIVE FINANCIAL MANAGEMENT IN THE CHURCH

The series of books of which this volume is a part is based on four major premises:

That if churches are to carry out their mission effectively, their business affairs must be managed as skillfully as those of other organizations;

That since churches are service-rendering rather than profit-making, their business policies and practices must differ in some respects from those of commercial enterprises, and that the differences must be identified;

That churches have opportunities and responsibilities for practicing, teaching, and recommending business procedures that their members may use appropriately and satisfactorily in the marketplace;

That helping people learn how to obtain and expend financial resources for the glory of God is a basic function of stewardship education.

Since churches are not profit-making, their budgetary procedures do differ in many respects from those of commercial enterprises. For example, budgeting in a commercial enterprise begins with a forecast of sales and an estimate of expense and cost of goods manufactured or otherwise acquired. Budgeting in a church begins with a forecast of needs to be met and programs to be accomplished. Inputs, such as labor, to the commercial enterprise, are paid for. Many of the most significant inputs to the church are volunteered. Much of financial planning in the business world is dominated by tax considerations. Churches, for the most part, are free of such concerns. Commercial enterprises are managed by owner-managers or hired professional managers. Management of churches is divided between ordained and volunteer or professional lay leadership.

However, the church can and should make full use of certain advanced and enlightened practices and procedures of private business and government. One such advance is the acceptance and use of budgeting as a management tool. The budget, whether in business or government or church, can no longer be a static or limiting document. It must be a flexible and responsive schedule developed as part of management and relating directly to planning, programming, and controlling the institution to which it pertains.

In fact, in many instances, because of prior connotations, the term "budgeting" has been dropped in favor of the term "resource programming." Consistent with this change in attitude, success in budgeting is not measured by the nearness of the ultimate result to that which was formerly budgeted. Rather, the success of the budget is measured by the degree to which it contributes to the attainment of the objectives.

Budgeting in a business enterprise reflects the needs of the business. These include: the need for profits, the need for sales by which such profits are generated, the need for labor and materials, the need for managerial and selling effort, the need for cash both for working purposes and for capital investment, and many other things. The overriding need is that of keeping sales, expenses, and profits in proper relation to one another.

Budgeting in government likewise reflects the needs of

the government: the need to fill the legislative, judicial, and administrative roles; the need to provide the services guaranteed to, or expected by, the citizenry; and the need for tax and other revenue with which all this is to be financed. Just as the business enterprise estimates and forecasts its capitalization and its costs of doing business in comparison to its sales revenue, the governmental unit forecasts its financial requirements for comparison with private and corporate income and the directly related tax resource.

In a similar manner, the imaginatively led church first estimates its needs, and only then turns to estimating its resources. This is a matter of attitude, of "state of mind," of approach. The church, business, or government that begins its financial planning by saying, "Our available resources are 'X dollars'; what can we buy with that amount?" will show little improvement, progress, or growth. They should say, "We need 'X dollars' to finance the things we wish to accomplish; how will we obtain the necessary money?"

What actually occurs is a sequence of phases in budget development during which successively revised estimates of needs and estimates of resources are brought closer and closer together. But, in each successive phase, the approach should be "programs and objectives first."

THE CONTEXT OF THE BUDGET

We have seen that church budgeting, when considered in its proper context, is part of the broad managerial function of planning, programming, and controlling the activity of a congregation. This context includes many other elements, some of which should be mentioned in this preliminary discussion. The budget must have a basis in policy. Much of policy is a matter of standards. For example, when the policy of the church is to pay local union scale wages to custodial employees, one can readily see how such a policy would influence the personnel and financial aspects of church management.

Another important element of the context of budgeting is the human factor. A healthy respect for the human factor must be present in every budget. The "human relations" phase of budgeting is as important as the technical aspect. The people concerned must feel that the budget is theirs; that they participated in its development; that they are contributors to the budget per se, and to the objectives that will be fulfilled. Anything that will be accomplished must be accomplished by people. The entire budgeting procedure should be carried out with this in mind.

THE COMPONENTS OF A COMPREHENSIVE BUDGET

We often speak of the church budget as though it were a single document. This is sometimes the case, in a relatively simple situation. More frequently, however, the church budget will consist of at least these four parts:

- The operating budget
- The capital budget
- The cash-flow budget
- The appeal budget

The first three are "working papers" used primarily by the church officers, committees, and staff. Their content and method of preparation will be taken up in detail in the chapters that follow.

The fourth, the appeal budget, is a membership and public release version, highlighting the program to be financed and describing in popular terms the expenses and resources visualized for the forthcoming fiscal period. This is the version of the budget used in the every-member-canvass and in other appeals for financial support.

Not components of the budget, but essential and directly related, are the financial accounting system and the reporting procedures and format used by the treasurer and financial secretary. So that maximum efficiency and effectiveness will be achieved, all of these should employ common language and the same sequence of recording. All should be coordinated in time so that current information can be used to mutual advantage by all concerned.

THE LANGUAGE OF BUDGETING

We see already that several terms have special meanings when used in planning and budgeting. Other terms that may be unfamiliar to some readers will appear in chapters which follow. Let us discuss them in related groups. As a convenience to the reader, these terms are included also in an easy-reference glossary in Appendix B, on page 177.

Effective church budgeting involves the use of four basic concepts: policy making, planning, programming, and controlling.

Policy making is the predetermination of the approach that will be taken to problems that might arise or situations that might be anticipated. Policies, in a sense, are attitudes.

There can be no such thing as policy after the fact. Policy must be developed beforehand, and then remembered or recorded for use when the anticipated situation arises. An example has already been noted of what a church policy might be in regard to payment of wages to custodial employees. Other policies might involve such matters as prepayment or anticipation of debt installments, or the manner in which unscheduled emergency costs of property maintenance might be met.

We have said that policy should be remembered or recorded. Churches should maintain a file of policies, and, at appropriate times, should publish pertinent policy items in newsletters and similar media addressed to their members.

Planning is the conscious process of selecting and systematically developing the best course of action to accomplish an objective. Planning must be consistent with policy. The two together—policy making and planning—form the foundation from which management springs. In addition to being consistent with policy, planning must reflect conditions that are either known, assumed, or visualized to exist.

In many cases, it is useful to distinguish between short-range, intermediate, and long-range plans. For example, a church's decision to provide within the new few months a series of lectures and seminars on problems of youth would certainly be a short-range plan. A proposal to adopt a new church school curriculum over the next two or three years would be a plan of an intermediate nature. Arrangements to build an addition to the sanctuary six, eight, or ten years in the future would be an example of long-range planning.

Programming follows planning and is the step between plans and the budget. Programs are detailed and time phased. Let us continue the previous example of the church's plan for revising its church school curriculum. The programs for accomplishing this plan would include the specific calendar periods in which each grade level of the church school is to be changed over, the number of students and teachers involved, the number of sets of instructional material needed, and the costs of such material in each period.

Controlling is the managerial process by which responsible individuals determine whether what was done during a period corresponded to the policies, plans, and programs that had been developed. Controlling, therefore, involves evaluating what has been done, comparing this with what was planned, and overcoming or correcting deficiencies and discrepancies found to exist.

These four managerial processes—policy making, planning, programming, and controlling—in many ways create a circle of activity. The conscious consideration of policy (that is, the predetermination of how we will react to various situations that occur), the planning based on those policies, and the programs detailing those plans—all must be developed in sequence and all must be evaluated. As a result of this evaluation (the control procedure), another cycle or round begins. New policies may be required, old policies may need to be revised, and plans and programs may need to be changed.

All policy making, planning, programming, and budgeting must be accomplished within a time frame. These time frames are referred to as periods: the operating period, the budgeting period, the programming period, and the planning period.

The *operating period* is a specified span of time (usually a year) in which we are gathering income, making expenditures, and accomplishing what was programmed to be accomplished.

The *budget period* (also usually a year) is the one for which we are now developing our budgets and which will begin on the day following the end of the operating period.

The *program period* is next in line. It is close enough so that we should be working in detail on the programs we wish to accomplish at that time in the life of our church.

The next phase is referred to as the *planning period*. This period, and the years that follow, are the ones we think of in our intermediate and long-range planning.

On any one day we are in all four time frames or periods. We are *operating* on the basis of the planning, programming, and budgeting done in past years. We are involved in *budgeting* for the following year, and in *programming* and *planning* against the years ahead. It may seem unnecessary or impractical to think in terms of three or four years into the future. We should continually be conscious of the future and should not allow policy making, planning, and programming decisions to pile up in the last few weeks or months before a budget must be prepared and adopted. Perhaps if we think in terms of budgeting, programming, and planning over a three-year span, we shall attain a happy compromise between accomplishment of these things over that long a period and crowding them into a few hectic weeks.

There are four terms that refer to the four budgetary documents or schedules. The first is the term *operating budget,* sometimes called the expense and revenue budget. The operating budget is a schedule of all incomes and expenses for a prescribed period, normally a year. The operating budget lists total amounts expected from pledges and offerings, as examples of items of income, and total amounts to be paid in salaries and utility bills, as examples of items of expense.

The *capital budget* contains all entries regarding the sources and uses of funds for purchase or construction of property and buildings, and for major items of equipment to be installed on the church property. For example, the purchase of real estate to be used as the site of a future parsonage, or the purchase of a new organ, are items included in the capital budget.

Another term, the *appeal budget,* is commonly used by churches and other voluntary organizations. The appeal budget is a separate document organized and worded in a manner useful and suitable in appealing for financial support of the church. The operating and capital budgets are detailed, with exact dollar-and-cents amounts and very likely employing language of the accounting system of the church. The appeal budget, by contrast, uses language of greater general interest. It does not contain details of routine expenses, but shows the major items in rounded-off figures that can be easily read and readily understood.

The fourth document is the financial budget, sometimes called the *financial plan* or *cash-flow schedule.* In contrast to the operating, capital, and appeal budgets, which show only total amounts for the entire period, the financial plan separates these amounts into quarterly, monthly, or weekly increments. Thus the financial plan is a forecast of income and expense on a week-to-week or month-to-month basis. It is the document that guides the church officials who are responsible for detailed financial management.

ADVANTAGES OF BUDGETING

Perhaps the greatest advantage of budgeting is that budgetary procedure forces responsible individuals into earlier consideration of the policies necessary, and the planning and programming needed to establish and attain the objectives of the church. Good budgetary procedure compels earlier and more intensive consideration of what must be done and what resources can be marshalled to aid in accomplishing the things necessary. It brings about an earlier recognition of organizational and financial weaknesses than would otherwise come about.

Secondly, budgeting requires adequate and meaningful organization. Budgeting can be accomplished only if assignment of responsibility for each function to be performed and objective to be reached is definitely made. The process of budgeting frequently discovers unassigned responsibilities, or, sometimes, duplicating responsibilities.

Budgeting increases participation in conducting the affairs of the church by involving many people in identifying and establishing goals or objectives and in planning the means of attaining them. Budgeting increases and improves co-ordination and harmony in the church. Good budgeting can be accomplished only in a co-operative and collaborative atmosphere.

Budgeting forces commitments. It requires that the things we talk about doing be set down in cold figures. At the same time, it promotes realism in that translating our ideas and objectives into dollars and dates guides us against unwarranted optimism or unjustified enthusiasm.

Budgeting compels a program or an activity to maintain adequate accounting for its financial and physical resources. It thus contributes to the effectiveness and orderliness with which these resources are managed, and to an increased consciousness of responsibility for proper application of church funds and materials. In this way, budgeting encourages economical use of money, labor, materials, and facilities. It serves as a force for conserving resources and applying them where intended.

The process of budgeting instills habits of timely, careful, and searching consideration of the various factors involved prior to the rendering of decisions. Through this more timely and adequate consideration, much uncertainty as to the capabilities and objectives of the church is removed from the minds of the church's leaders and participating members and friends.

The control phase of budgeting forces a periodic and critical analysis of accomplishments. This is useful not only in identifying areas where more emphasis is currently required but also in planning for future periods. This self-analysis gauges progress not only in gathering and applying resources, but also in attaining objectives.

Lastly, and perhaps of more tangible value, the fact that the church pursues sound budgetary practices is of interest to creditors. It is a point favoring loans and grants when these are being considered by loan institutions and foundation officers and directors.

COMMON FAULTS AND LIMITATIONS IN BUDGETING

Sometimes church budgeting is not successful, or is successful only to a degree. This is attributable primarily to two causes. The first is that those in charge of budgeting do not support the program and budget, or perhaps they support it in some areas and circumvent it in others. Secondly, those involved in conducting the affairs of the church do not appreciate the limitations of budgeting.

Attempts at church budgeting have failed in many instances because those concerned expected too much. In other cases, the system of budgeting was installed too rapidly, without due regard for the length of time necessary to develop understanding on the part of the many individuals concerned. In some instances, the organizational structure and the placement of authority were not compatible with the type of budgeting attempted. In other cases, the accounting system and the records maintained were not adequate to support a meaningful planning and programming process. In many cases, the persons involved in budgeting did not follow through to the final necessary step of budgetary control and to an analysis of results and a correction of discrepancies and deficiencies. In still other examples, the budgetary process was too detailed, the real meaning of the budget being buried in a mass of relatively unimportant figures.

Successful budgeting depends on the basic soundness of the budgetary system and its understanding and acceptance by the personnel concerned. The budget that is understandable avoids unnecessary details and complications. Budgets should be kept simple, highlighting significant items and merging and consolidating minor and recurring items.

Aside from the various factors leading to failure of a budgetary effort, there are at least four basic limitations that must be borne in mind.

First, a budget is an estimate or a projection. It can only be as good as the experience and assumptions upon which it is based.

Secondly, a budget is valid only as of the instant it was completed and approved. It must be a dynamic and flexible document, subject to reconsideration and amendment as circumstances change.

Thirdly, the actions and programs budgeted will not be put into effect automatically. The fact that they are included in the budget, and have been accepted and approved by the congregation, means only that their accomplishment is intended. They will have to be implemented by individual action of each contributing organization.

Lastly, a budget does not take the place of management. It is merely another tool of management and is to be used together with all the other human and quantitative tools available to the leadership of the church.

DEPARTMENTAL BUDGETS
AND UNIFIED BUDGETS

The first decision in church budgeting is the choice between a comprehensive master budget, commonly called a "unified budget," and a series of separate organizational or departmental budgets.

Under the departmental budget approach, each activity having a source of income makes its own decision as to how that income is to be spent. Under a unified budget, all income goes into a common fund and all is considered available to apply against the broad inclusive needs of the church.

Although the unified budget is widely used and generally recognized as best meeting the total needs and resources of the local church, it is not uncommon to find individual organizational budgeting. Combinations of the two approaches are common.

Some churches seem to believe they have a unified budget because all the income and expense of its organizations appear in more or less uniform form in the church financial or accounting records. To be truly unified, the various activities must not only treat their programming and budgeting similarly, but must all be subject to church-wide decision-making in the process.

The choice between the departmental approach and the unified approach to church budget development should be made on the basis of denominational and local feelings.

Departmental budgets, traditional in many churches, frequently are retained because of values found in the closer ties that develop when individuals or groups within the church make significant financial contributions. The fact that a ladies' guild or a men's Bible class not only supports itself but makes an organizational pledge to the central expense of the church is important from the morale point of view. Departmental budgeting probably encourages a form of participation in church life that may be lost when groups lose their financial independence.

But unified budgeting implies more than mere uniformity in procedure and a church-wide approach to expenditure decisions. It means that the congregation is united in its effort to provide material resources for the church. It means also that the entire congregation can participate in determining the application of those resources. Under the departmental or organizational budget, the really essential and basic needs of the church may be neglected in favor of an expenditure for something considered important by one organization. One example is the church with the run-down sanctuary and wheezy organ, but with a gleaming modern kitchen, because the ladies' guild was determined to spend "its money" on the kitchen.

Since the unified budget has much in its favor and is now most widely used, this book deals largely with church budgeting under the unified approach.

Confusion between departmental budgets and unified budgets need not arise because of the fact that the unified budget may be instituted along organizational lines. There are only two ways a church budget may be subdivided into understandable and useful parts. One of these is organizational, the other functional. In an organizational budget the headings usually consist of organizational names, such as "Board of Religious Education," with subheadings covering each of the programs coming under that board's responsibilities and authority. In a functional budget, the headings indicate functions to be performed, such as "Property Maintenance and Provision of Utilities." Subheadings cover each object for which expenditures are anticipated: landscaping and lawn care, cleaning and redecorating, heating, lighting, and others.

In the church where every task and every program is under the surveillance of some department, board, committee, or council, an organizational structure is appropriate. In the appeal budget, however (as will be explored at greater length in Chapter 6), identification of functions to be performed is far more important than identification of spending organizations.

THE REALITY OF THE CHURCH BUDGET

The programs of the church begin as ideas, as discussions among its members. They start to take on reality when they are included in an operating budget or capital budget. They become almost real when the budget is approved and subscribed. They actually come about when the responsible members, using the authority to act and the resources contained in the budget, go ahead and do what they set out to do.

Just as programs are not real until they are budgeted, budgets are not real unless they are a true reflection of the church's programs.

Other things add to the reality of the church budget. The first of these is the element of individual involvement, one of the human factors mentioned earlier. A sufficient part of the membership must participate in developing the budget, and enough must attend meetings where it is discussed and voted upon, to have it reach a point where it can really be felt that a personal commitment has been effected. Finally, the budget must have a specific moment of approval, a date on which the total membership or a truly representative body says, "This is our approved program and budget for the forthcoming year."

In the next chapter, we will consider further such questions as: "How does the budget relate to the plans, programs, and objectives of the church?" "Who is responsible for program and budget development?" "What should be the beginning and ending dates of the church's fiscal period?" "What are the criteria of successful church budgeting?"

Chapter 2

PLANNING, COORDINATING, AND CONTROLLING

ESSENTIALS FOR EFFECTIVE BUDGETING

SUCCESSFUL CHURCH BUDGET development depends on a great many factors, of which at least four are essential:

• There must be some formal organization, at least enough to identify (trace) responsibility for the many programs and functions of the church.

• There must be a framework of programming and budgeting procedure.

• There must be participation in the budgetary process by as large a group as possible, and there must be general appreciation of what is being attempted.

• There must be appraisal of accomplishments and institution of corrective action when needed.

Church business management can become more effective through better planning, coordination, and control. Effective coordination of the human and material resources of the church depends largely on sound planning beforehand and prompt control while the activity is going on. These three managerial functions—planning, coordination, and control—are facilitated by the use of the budget.

In relating planning to budgeting, we must first distinguish between forecasting and planning. Forecasting is our best thinking or our best judgment as to what will happen in the future. Planning, by contrast, is what we believe we can cause to happen in the future.

Forecasting is a basis of planning. We have said earlier that we must either establish on some factual basis what we believe will come about in future periods, or we must make an assumption as to what we believe will come about. Whether based upon factual information or upon assumption, it is still a forecast.

In relating the planning function to budgeting, there are several distinct connections. The plans must be measured in terms of money. The plans must be weighed in dollar terms against many other aspects, such as the human aspects previously discussed. Also, budgeting helps provide a choice between alternatives that may have developed in our planning. Lastly, both the planning and budgeting must make allowances for what can be done if things work out differently from what was forecast.

Developing a plan and converting it into dollar amounts necessitates a high degree of coordination among all concerned. The entire process goes very smoothly when mutual confidence and understanding exist and when the various roles are clearly defined and understood. From this point of view, budgeting forces the establishment and maintenance of person-to-person relationships. This means a great deal more than merely identifying responsibilities in organizational directives or organization charts.

Budgeting is also a very effective tool for use in the managerial function of control. Control is based upon certain essentials and can be successful only when these essentials are met: first, there must be a sound statement of goals to be achieved or standards to be met, upon which to base control action; second, there must be an accurate record of what was actually accomplished; third, there must be a careful comparison of actual performance with what was planned; and lastly, this action must be carefully evaluated and corrective action promptly taken.

Control should take the form of periodic and interim reporting by the various activities, the analysis of variations and, where indicated, the revision of the budget in terms of budget flexibility. Control works best when it develops as a disciplined effort to follow a plan or budget and to explain the deviations from the plan or budget. This effort should be voluntary, unified, and cooperative.

Deviations from a plan or budget should be discussed beforehand and authorized by responsible individuals. If the deviation cannot be prevented, as for example the failure of some expected contribution to materialize, the situation is at least spotlighted as early as possible so that the necessary action may be taken. Such an attitude toward control is often spoken of as "management by exception." This term implies that activities planned and budgeted for are assumed to be going on, and only when deviations are desired or cannot be prevented is an exception created which calls for managerial action.

RESPONSIBILITY FOR BUDGET DEVELOPMENT

Because of considerable variety of organizational form in local churches of the several denominations, there are wide differences in the designation of groups responsible for the budgetary process. To avoid confusion, we shall consistently use the term "board" to mean a permanently standing organization legally created by the constitution of the church, or by similar authority. The members of a board normally are elected to that membership. We shall use the term "committee" as meaning a group appointed to deal with specific matters brought before it. A committee may be disbanded when it has completed its assigned task.

Many of the boards, committees, and individuals with whom we shall be concerned have responsibilities beyond programming and budgeting. Appendix C, page 181, may be referred to for general descriptions of duties and responsibilities.

A common unit of church organization is the board of finance. Ideally, this group should be chosen by the congregation on a staggered-term basis so that a continuity of policies and procedures may be maintained. The size of the group, of course, would vary with the duties normally expected.

In the author's church, the members of the board of finance, in pairs, actually receive, count, and record the Sunday offerings. To do this on an equitable basis, which in this case means one Sunday a month, a membership of eight individuals plus a chairman and the church financial secretary and treasurer make up the board. The board is responsible for conducting the annual cycle of budgeting and the continuing study of accomplishment of the annual program, to the extent that it is measurable in dollar terms. In other words, the board of finance maintains a year-round review of the financial management of the church. As part of this review, each report of the treasurer and the financial secretary is studied for approval.

The role of the board of finance in budget development and budgetary control is that of:

• Establishing procedures for developing the church program and budget;

• Promulgating the financial policy of the church as handed down by the board of deacons, the church council, the pastor, and others in policy-making positions;

• Establishing the timetable of program and budget development and implementation;

• Authorizing and controlling expenditures, and monitoring their conformance with the budget;

• Delegating authority to approve expenditures, in conformance with church policy;

• Reporting periodically on the accomplishment of the program and budget.

While the board of finance is responsible for establishing and conducting the church's budgetary process, the actual work of preparing the budget should be done by a separately appointed programs-and-budget committee, chosen each year from the major groups having financial needs to be met. The chairman of the board of finance, or his appointed representative, should be a key member of the programs and budget committee. The pastor should be either a member of the committee or an observer at most of its meetings.

In Chapter 5, a schedule for accomplishing the annual budgeting process is proposed. That schedule shows at what time of the year the programs-and-budget committee must be convened and at what time its work should be completed. Basically, the committee's task consists of receiving the estimates of needs and income from the various operating groups of the church, reconciling any differences or problems in regard to these submissions, and combining the whole into a well-stated and understandable program and budget. The committee should schedule a series of open meetings, or "hearings," at which heads of various departments and programs discuss their respective needs and budget proposals. Although the committee may be satisfied to receive these proposals orally, better management practice would require their being submitted in writing on a simple standard format.

A report on the programs-and-budget committee's deliberations should eventually be made to the highest organizational element in the local church—the board of deacons or the church council, depending on its designation. Upon acceptance of this report, the committee should be thanked and dismissed. Thereafter, throughout the operating period, the board of finance is charged with program and budget responsibility as it accomplishes the function we have described as budgetary control.

The church treasurer plays an important role in budget development by providing factual information as to actual receipts and disbursements in periods past and the purpose for which such disbursements were made. His records provide the foundation from which forecasts may be made. The church treasurer, perhaps with the assistance of the church office staff, should provide this information in comparative summary form, so that the various objects for which expenses were incurred over a period of several years may be reviewed simultaneously. The financial secretary's records are used in a manner similar to those of the church treasurer.

The temptation arises, particularly in the smaller churches, but also in the larger organization with a paid, full-time treasurer, to ask the church treasurer to compile the budget. Obviously, much is lost when this is done. The budget should be a participation project for as many members of the congregation as can be effectively employed in its development. In this way, true concern and interest are encouraged on a broader basis. The budget developed by a single individual is likely to be little more than a simple projection into the future of current needs and resources. Program and budget development is a task for the entire leadership of the church.

The role of the pastor or rabbi in budget development is highly important. He must establish and promote the idea of stewardship in the minds of all who participate in the program and budget work. He must provide spiritual and practical guidance to the programs-and-budget committee and to the board of finance. He must state his own needs, and his opinion of the relative value and importance of the programs to be financed. In addition, he must assure the participation and assistance of the church staff in the work of preparing the budget.

PROJECTING THE FUTURE OF THE
INDIVIDUAL CHURCH

It is a common practice among many kinds of institutions and agencies to project the future of the organization in rather simple terms. For example, a business firm may project its size in terms of capitalized value. In other instances, a business may project its future in terms of anticipated volume of sales. This may be stated either in absolute dollar amounts or in terms of a percentage of the market in which the company is participating. Most successful companies engage in such practices, and, more important, subject themselves to a hard-boiled self-analysis if they fall short of their stated objectives.

Certainly a church can do no less than project itself into at least a mid-range planning period. In a fine example of such a projection, the Aldersgate Methodist Church of Alexandria, Virginia, projected its future in half-yearly increments for three years. (See Exhibit 1, on page 40.) Their study included a projection of members in terms of the beginning membership, anticipated change of membership, and expected ending membership for each period. The projection also shows the total amount of the church's operating and capital budgets, together with the various sources of income, major expenses, and cash balances, on both a period and cumulative basis.

The Commission of Stewardship of the Lutheran Church in America recommends a similar procedure and furnishes a series of forms designed to facilitate identification of trends in the local parish. Parts of that procedure are included here as Exhibit 2, beginning on page 41. The use of techniques such as illustrated by Exhibits 1 and 2 is highly recommended.

Exhibit 1. Example of a Projection of Church Membership, Income and Expenses.

(Based upon a format developed and successfully used by the Aldersgate Methodist Church of Alexandria, Virginia.)

PROJECTION OF MEMBERSHIP, INCOME AND EXPENSES

	Description	Actual 12-1-56 to 5-31-56	Actual 6-1-57 to 11-30-57	Actual 12-1-57 to 5-31-58	Estimated 6-1-58 to 11-30-58	Estimated 12-1-58 to 5-31-59	Estimated 6-1-59 to 11-30-59	Estimated 12-1-59 to 5-31-60	Estimated 6-1-60 to 11-30-60	Estimated 12-1-60 to 5-31-61
	MEMBERSHIP									
1.										
2.	Beginning of period	52	74	96	123	150	180	220	260	300
3.	Increase	22	22	27	27	30	40	40	40	40
4.	End of period	74	96	123	150	180	220	260	300	340
5.	Average	63	85	109	136	165	200	240	280	320
6.	**CONTRIBUTIONS & OTHER RECEIPTS**									
7.	For current expenses	$ 1,559	$ 2,135	$ 2,573	$ 3,375	$ 4,084	$ 4,950	$ 5,940	$ 6,930	$ 7,920
8.	For building fund – local	1,555	2,042	2,648	3,382	4,084	4,950	5,940	6,930	7,920
9.	– Board of Missions	-	-	2,000	3,000	20,000	30,000	-	-	-
10.	– loan	-	-	-	-	25,000	-	-	-	-
11.	TOTAL	3,114	4,177	7,221	9,750	53,168	39,900	11,880	13,860	15,840
12.	Cumulative – current expenses	1,798	3,933	6,506	9,881	13,965	18,915	24,855	31,785	39,705
13.	– building fund	1,580	3,622	8,270	14,652	63,736	98,686	104,626	111,556	119,476
14.	TOTAL	3,378	7,555	14,776	24,533	77,701	117,601	129,481	143,341	159,181
15.	**EXPENSES**									
16.	For current expenses	1,091	2,485	2,441	3,300	4,000	4,900	5,900	6,900	7,100
17.	For building fund	-	-	4,790	3,400	51,900	37,150	6,000	6,000	6,000
18.	TOTAL	1,091	2,485	7,231	6,700	55,900	42,050	11,900	12,900	13,100
19.	Cumulative – current expenses	1,091	3,576	6,017	9,317	13,317	18,217	24,117	31,017	38,117
20.	– building fund	-	-	4,790	8,190	60,090	97,240	103,240	109,240	115,240
21.	TOTAL	$ 1,091	$ 3,576	$ 10,807	$ 17,507	$ 73,407	$ 115,457	$ 127,357	$ 140,257	$ 153,357

PARISH TRENDS ... in our MISSION

	3 Years Ago 19........	2 Years Ago 19........	Last Year 19........	Trend +	Trend −	Trend O	Projection

MEMBERSHIP:

Baptized Membership ....
Confirmed Membership ....
Confirmed Membership in Good Standing ....
Communing Membership ....
Percent of Confirmed Communing ....
Membership Gained ....
Membership Losses ....
Prospective Members ....
Youth in Armed Services ....
Youth in Colleges ....

WORSHIP:

Average Attendance per Sunday ....
Number of Children Attending ....
Per cent Baptized Membership Attending ....
Per cent Confirmed Membership Attending ....

CHRISTIAN EDUCATION:

Sunday Church School Pupils ....
Released Time School Pupils ....
Vacation Church School Pupils ....
Confirmation Class Pupils ....
Adult Classes ....
Teachers in Service ....
Teachers in Training ....
Classes without Teachers ....

AGE GROUP ANALYSIS:

Number	Group	% of Total
	1 to 15	
	16 to 20	
	21 to 30	
	31 to 40	
	41 to 50	
	51 to 60	
	61 to 70	
	71 and over	
Note how effectively each group is being served.		

LEADERSHIP DISTRIBUTION:

Number of Organizations ....
Number of Committees ....
Number of ....
    Total Organizational Complex ....
_____Persons with one local leadership responsibility
_____Persons with two local leadership responsibilties
_____Persons with three local leadership responsibilities
_____Persons with four local leadership responsibilities
_____different persons serving_____leadership roles.
Our confirmed membership is_____.

SONS AND DAUGHTERS IN CHURCH OCCUPATIONS:

Our congregation is_____years old. In that time_____ men have been channeled into the ministry and_____members into other full time church occupations. The total includes_____within the past five years.

OUR COMMUNITY:

According to 19____census figures there are_____people in our area. We are serving_____%.

Exhibit 2. Examples of Worksheets for Studying Parish Trends

(Three pages from *Parish Trends—A Workbook for the Research Committee,* written by Walter A. Jensen. Produced and distributed by the Commission on Stewardship and the Lutheran Layman's Movement for Stewardship of the Lutheran Church in America.)

PARISH TRENDS... in our CORPORATE STEWARDSHIP

ANNUAL OFFERINGS:

	3 Years Ago 19........	2 Years Ago 19........	Last Year 19........	Trend +	−	O
Weekly Envelopes:						
Current Expenses						
Apportioned Benevolences						
Unapportioned Benevolences						
Loose Plate						
Other (except receipts for unusual expenses, buildings, transfers, etc.)						
Total Normal Receipts						
Add: Other Income (Building, etc.)						
TOTAL RECEIPTS						

Comparison Averages per Confirmed Member						
Our Congregation						
LCA						
Our Synod						

ANNUAL EXPENDITURES:

Current Expenses						
Apportioned Benevolences						
Unapportioned Benevolences						
Unusual Expenses						
TOTAL EXPENDITURES						

Average per Confirmed Member						
Current Expenses						
Unusual Expenses						
Apportioned Benevolences						
Unapportioned Benevolences						
TOTAL EXPENDITURES PER MEMBER						
Percentage of Income for Benevolence Purposes	%	%	%			
Total Amount Pledged						
Total Pledges Received						
Percent "Shrinkage"	%	%	%			

OUR WORSHIP AND SERVICE FACILITIES:

Physical Property:	Date Acquired	Original Cost	Est. Cost to Replace	Insured for
The Church Building				
The Parish Hall				
The Parsonage				
Other				

INDEBTEDNESS:

Loan Represented by:	Original Date	Original Amount	Now Owing	Interest Rate	Accumulated Interest Paid
1.				%	
2.				%	
3.				%	

Exhibit 2.   Continued

PARISH TRENDS ... *in our INDIVIDUAL STEWARDSHIP*

Determine the pattern of giving on a weekly basis per contributor. This is done by finding the total gift for the year of each person or couple to whom envelopes were issued. Divide by 52 to arrive at the *average weekly gift.* If a husband and wife contribute through one envelope, divide by 2 to arrive at the individual figure and count them as 2 contributors. Make one study of total giving for current and benevolence causes, another for benevolences alone. If capital gifts are currently being given, make a separate study of these.

For Current Expenses and Benevolences	For Benevolences Only
_____ gave . . . . . . over $25.00 per week	_____ gave . . . . . . over $25.00 per week
_____ gave . . . . $20.01 to $25.00 per week	_____ gave . . . . $20.01 to $25.00 per week
_____ gave . . . . 15.01 to 20.00 per week	_____ gave . . . . 15.01 to 20.00 per week
_____ gave . . . . 12.51 to 15.00 per week	_____ gave . . . . 12.51 to 15.00 per week
_____ gave . . . . 10.01 to 12.50 per week	_____ gave . . . . 10.01 to 12.50 per week
_____ gave . . . . 7.51 to 10.00 per week	_____ gave . . . . 7.51 to 10.00 per week
_____ gave . . . . 5.01 to 7.50 per week	_____ gave . . . . 5.01 to 7.50 per week
_____ gave . . . . 4.01 to 5.00 per week	_____ gave . . . . 4.01 to 5.00 per week
_____ gave . . . . 3.01 to 4.00 per week	_____ gave . . . . 3.01 to 4.00 per week
_____ gave . . . . 2.01 to 3.00 per week	_____ gave . . . . 2.01 to 3.00 per week
_____ gave . . . . 1.51 to 2.00 per week	_____ gave . . . . 1.51 to 2.00 per week
_____ gave . . . . 1.01 to 1.50 per week	_____ gave . . . . 1.01 to 1.50 per week
_____ gave . . . . .76 to 1.00 per week	_____ gave . . . . .76 to 1.00 per week
_____ gave . . . . .51 to .75 per week	_____ gave . . . . .51 to .75 per week
_____ gave . . . . .26 to .50 per week	_____ gave . . . . .26 to .50 per week
_____ gave . . . . .05 to .25 per week	_____ gave . . . . .05 to .25 per week
_____ gave . . . . nothing per week	_____ gave . . . . nothing per week
_____ TOTAL	_____ TOTAL

ANALYSIS OF THIS YEAR'S WEEKLY PLEDGES FOR CURRENT EXPENSES AND BENEVOLENCES

Weekly Pledge	Insert Exact Number of Persons				Persons		Total Pledged Weekly	
	1 - 10	11 - 25	26 - 50	Over 50	Total	%	Dollars	%
Over $25.00								
20.01 to 25.00								
15.01 to 20.00								
12.51 to 15.00								
10.01 to 12.50								
7.51 to 10.00								
5.01 to 7.50								
4.01 to 5.00								
3.01 to 4.00								
2.01 to 3.00								
1.51 to 2.00								
1.01 to 1.50								
.76 to 1.00								
.51 to .75								
.26 to .50								
.05 to .25								
Nothing								
						100%		100%

Contributions pledged for _____ months . . . . $_____
Pledged Income received—same period . . . . $_____
There are _____ envelope sets in use, and we have _____ confirmed members.

Exhibit 2. Continued

THE FISCAL PERIOD

The period of time encompassed by a church budget or financial plan is usually called the "fiscal year." When should the fiscal year begin, and when should it end? What factors should we consider in establishing the inclusive dates of the budget period?

The fiscal year for the individual local church should be designated with regard to the conditions and activities peculiar to that church. It should not be selected for purely arbitrary reasons. One of the features of the fiscal year is that it can disregard the calendar year. It can begin and end on any convenient dates, and, although not the usual practice, it can extend for more or less than 12 months.

As an example, the fiscal year of a university normally begins the first of September and continues through the end of August. This is commensurate with the pattern of receipts and expenditures of a university and with the concept of the academic year. The fiscal year of automobile manufacturers normally closes during September, which fits the pattern of the yearly close-out of previous models and the introduction of new models.

The fiscal year of the Federal Government runs from the first of July to the thirtieth of the following June. The fiscal years of industries concerned with agricultural products, such as canners of fruits and vegetables, generally end in February, as do those of many building contractors. Reasons behind the selection of these terminal dates involve a combination of seasonal considerations and the closely related matter of availability of work time in which to accomplish programming and budgeting actions.

The fiscal year of a local church might well be established on the basis of similar reasoning. Summer usually is a slack period in church activity, yet it is a period of limited availability of members to participate. Principal religious observances of the church, such as Christmas and Easter, and other holidays and anniversaries, will also affect the decision. Certainly there would seem to be some wisdom in avoiding the calendar year, January 1st to December 31st, as the church fiscal year. Using the calendar year as a fiscal year means that much time-consuming work of developing and considering the church budget will take place during the busy Thanksgiving and Christmas seasons.

The pattern of church activities and the availability of responsible people would seem to indicate that a fiscal period terminating in the early summer is most appropriate. Thus, much of the budget preparation could be done following Easter, and in time for a fiscal year beginning in June or July. Accordingly, the financial period would begin in the low income portion of the year, the summer vacation months, and would terminate in the higher income months of the spring. This, in turn, would allow greater flexibility in the budget and would ease recovery from periods of peak expenditure. Whatever the program and budget period is, the accounting period must correspond.

The budget period need not necessarily be 12 months. There may be reasons why a particular church should have a longer period or a shorter one. However, the longer the budget period, the greater is the chance that plans and programs will be upset as time passes and conditions and influences change. On the other hand, a budget period that is too short runs the risk of failing to take into account important events that may lie just beyond the budget period. Those who have experimented with short—less than 12-month—budget periods usually have concluded that it takes considerably less effort to prepare a budget annually.

The fiscal period of some churches is dictated by higher denominational authority. Often a conference or district will ask that all member churches use the same fiscal year. Where this is done merely for administrative convenience, the progressive individual church should request either more appropriate timing or greater flexibility.

THE CONTINUUM OF PROGRAMS AND BUDGETS

Sometimes we may tend to think of budget periods as individual blocks of time beginning and ending on some carefully chosen dates. Each annual budget should not be thought of as standing alone. Rather, the whole planning, programming, and budgeting process should be viewed as a continuum, rolling on year after year. Each successive plan, program, and budget should be related to each other. Many plans or programs will not be completed in a single year's time; therefore, each year is but a single link in a chain of activity.

Each annual increment should begin with the residue of the preceding increment. The work remaining to be done, the assets remaining unused, the bills remaining unpaid—all of these carry over into the next succeeding budget. Whether these resources and liabilities continue to be treated as if they were still part of the preceding year, or are reconsidered as part of the new year, depends upon whether the church visualizes certain of its items as being what the Bureau of the Budget calls "no-year money," money that is available at any time until it is used. Most churches will find it is best not to follow this concept. Resources remaining at the end of a year should come up for reconsideration for use in the new period.

CRITERIA OF SUCCESSFUL BUDGETING

The budget must not be given importance beyond what it deserves; its power must not be overemphasized. It must not be used as an excuse for failing to accomplish a desired end, nor as an easy way of rejecting a proposal requiring financial resources. The budget is a plan and an authorization, subject to change as the situation changes, and flexible enough to respond to emergencies and unforeseen circumstances.

Success in church budgeting is not measured by the ultimate similarity of the result to what was budgeted. It is measured by the degree to which the programs and objectives established by the church are attained.

In Chapter 3, we will begin our detailed consideration of the budget, answering questions such as: "How are proposed expenditures developed and presented for incorporation into the budget?" and, "What are some of the major considerations in analyzing program and budget submissions?"

Part II

The Church Budget
in Preparation

IDENTIFYING AND ANALYZING FINANCIAL NEEDS OF CHURCHES

THIS CHAPTER IS concerned with determining and evaluating the financial needs of churches. Chapter 4 will discuss resources, and Chapter 5 will bring the needs and resources together into a working paper. Details of developing budget documents are considered in Chapter 5, "Preparing and Processing Budget Working Papers," and Chapter 6, "Preparing the Appeal Budget."

Our immediate objective is to identify each item of need that must be considered. This is the beginning of our unified plan of expenditures.

DISCRETIONARY AND NONDISCRETIONARY ITEMS OF EXPENSE

Most items of expense appearing in church budgets could be classified in many ways. For instance, they could be divided into two categories, "fixed" items and "variable" items, because some of them remain more or less fixed and consistent over the years, whereas others vary considerably from period to period. This distinction is useful in the discussion and study of individual items of the budget. However, few items should continue the same year after year. Most entries reflect a pattern of change as objectives and conditions change.

Usually the items of need or expense can be divided into two groups, using the labels "discretionary" and "nondiscretionary." It is easiest to itemize the nondiscretionary items first. These include established salaries of the staff, and related expenses such as allowances and annuities. They include also any assessments over which the church has little or no control. Still other such items include financial and legal obligations, interest on debts, and dated commitments for repayment of principal.

Discretionary items are those over which the officers and staff of the church do have control. Improvements and certain types of maintenance of the church property are discretionary. All elements of service and most departmental programs are discretionary in the sense that responsible individuals can decide whether they are to be underwritten.

Some items seem to defy classification as discretionary or nondiscretionary, because some of them might be thought of as discretionary only at certain points in time. A choice might exist on one date, but, having made that choice, the church is committed for a considerable period. For example, an item such as telephone expenses is discretionary. A church may decide to have minimum telephone service, a single instrument in the church office, or it might decide to have a great number of telephones with a switchboard and an intercommunication panel. At the time the installation is being considered, discretion exists as to how extensive a telephone system is necessary; but once the decision is made and the instruments installed, the economics of the case usually dictate that the service be continued, and the expense in following year becomes nondiscretionary.

Of course, expense items are not listed in budget documents as discretionary or nondiscretionary. Instead, this is part of the consideration of the items and the sequence in which they are studied. Generally, it is best to first enter on the working papers the amounts for the nondiscretionary items, taking the approach that these, for the most part, represent commitments that will be changed only if absolutely necessary. When all nondiscretionary items are listed on the working papers, a totaling of the items will give a preliminary indication of how far the church can go in financing discretionary expenses.

STUDY OF SIGNIFICANT AREAS OF NEED

As the programs-and-budget committee begins its work, it reviews the various areas of existing need, such as:

Pastoral leadership

Administrative and staff

Religious education

Participation in benevolences and charities

Commitment to denominational apportionments

Property maintenance

Promotional activities

Debt retirement and service

Expense for each area of need should be subjected to certain questions and comparisons. Experience of last year as well as that of the current operating period should be considered. Analysis of each area of need must be a function of the pertinent committee or board. This is basic. The programs-and-budget committee or the board of finance should, in receiving a budget request, be assured that a detailed study of the items included was made before the request was transmitted. It is important that boards and committees inform the program-and-budget committee of the true range of their considerations so that decisions will not be made on a dollar basis alone. The format for submitting budget requests should provide space for indicating the considerations taken into account in arriving at necessity and cost of each major item. A simple form adequately serving this purpose is shown on page 54, Exhibit 3.

_____
(date)

Memorandum for Chairman, Board of Finance

    The_____ submits the
          (name of board or committee)

following program information and budget estimate for the

year 1964.

    1. Basic Programs and Activities

Item	Estimated expense $
Sub total	$

    2. Special Programs and Proposed New Activities

Item	Estimated expense $
Sub total	$
' Total estimated expenses	$

    3. Revenue to the Church

Source	Estimated amounts $
Total estimated revenue	$

_____
(signed - chairman)

Exhibit 3. Example of a Format for Submission of Budget Estimate

COMPENSATION FOR THE PASTOR
AND THE CHURCH STAFF

Recommendations for compensation of the pastor and the church staff should clearly indicate that serious consideration has been given to such significant questions as: How does the salary of the pastor and his associates or assistants compare with salaries paid other professional people in the community? How closely should the pastor's salary parallel those of other professional groups in the community? Can the pastor maintain the public and social position that the church desires on the income he receives? What equivalent values in allowances and benefits does the pastor receive that are not normally received by other professional people —for example, the equivalent value of the parsonage and the church-financed car? Do salaries of pastor and staff bear a positive relationship to changes in the cost of living in the local area?

A report by the National Council of Churches, quoted widely in the daily papers and news magazines of May 1961, stated that the average cash salaries of Protestant ministers was $4,500 a year for a workweek ranging from 60 to 80 hours. To this is added an average annual allowance of $1,500 for housing and other expenses.

Average salaries reported by the National Council of Churches do not reflect successful efforts of many congregations to improve the lot of their ministers, not only in basic salary, but also in benefits ranging from tax-free housing to book allowances. These individual efforts are reflected in a September 1962 survey by *Time* magazine in which the average minimum pay for priests in the Southern Ohio Diocese of the Episcopal Church was reported as $8,000—an increase of $3,000 in the last decade. *Time* also reported that the average ministerial salary (including housing allowance) in the American Baptist Convention had risen to $5,705, and noted a report by the United Lutheran Church that the number of its clergymen earning less than $3,000 had dropped to 20 and the number earning $10,000 had risen to more than 85.

These are encouraging developments, representing a real awareness on the part of individual congregations, and a reflection of this awareness in their budgetary considerations. Also reported was a trend toward standardization of ministerial salaries, particularly in the Episcopal, Presbyterian, and the American Baptist churches. Even with such standardization, the responsibility remains for the individual church to give full consideration to all local community influences in establishing the rate of pastoral pay. Of course, a clergyman does not look primarily for material rewards, but he certainly must receive enough remuneration to make his life relatively free of economic problems or worries that tend to decrease his effectiveness.

Similar considerations arise in the matter of the salary scale for members of the church staff. Here, our analysis should perhaps be even more responsive to the local situation. In every locality, there are standards as to pay and hours for various types of duties. Ideally, the church should set an example in respecting such standards, but there is reason to suspect that such is generally not the case. The May 1961 study previously mentioned reported that church janitors and sextons working full time, or very nearly so, average wages of $2,500, with church secretaries and office workers averaging $2,800. It is hard to visualize these amounts as reflecting local consciousness of the "going wage" in most cities and neighborhoods.

RELIGIOUS EDUCATION

In the area of religious education, many considerations must be raised and resolved before a budgetary request can be made. Considerations involving compensation of a director of religious education or a paid superintendent should follow the pattern discussed in regard to pastoral leadership and church staff. Beyond this, the program should be based on the number of people to be reached. Many churches find it practical to base their analysis on a cost per individual —a figure developed over the years, including the cost of teaching aids, classroom supplies, and presentation Bibles. Other activities of the board of education should be handled on an item-by-item estimate. For example, a program of teacher recognition, perhaps including a banquet, should appear in the budget as a separate item at a stated cost. The same treatment should be given to special lectures or seminar programs offered by the board. Other programs falling within the discretionary group should be similarly treated because discretion may have to be exercised and some items reduced in scope or eliminated.

BENEVOLENCES AND CHARITIES

Under this heading are included such items as apportionments for benevolent purposes, support of social services, aid to church-related institutions, and often a discretionary benevolence fund to be used by the pastor as he sees fit and without accounting. The basic approach in budgeting benevolences should be to weigh these items, as an outreach program, against the internal needs of the local church. Many churches list benevolences first in their budget documents, as an indication that this is their highest consideration, and only after benevolences and charities are taken care of do they turn their attention to their own congregation.

Budgeting of benevolences and charities should be approached according to the discretionary and nondiscretionary concept previously described. Certainly those nondiscretionary benevolences and charities to which the local churches are committed, either by denominational authority or by their own prior agreement, should be set down early in the budgetary process. Discretionary benevolences and charities, however, should await their turn for consideration along with other discretionary items. Some questions that might be asked are: Does the amount proposed for benevolences outside our own church family reflect our true concern for the wants and problems of others at home and abroad? Does the amount proposed for benevolences place a strain on our financial situation, entailing some sacrifice on our part, or is it merely an easy figure that remains after everything else is taken care of? Certainly it should not be. In cases where perhaps we cannot do as much as we would like, have we at least included a token amount to show our interest and moral support? This is particularly appropriate on the local scene in that it demonstrates our concern with the lot of our neighbors.

Probably the most controversial item in this group is the pastor's discretionary fund. There have been instances of a pastor's discretionary fund being used to support activities not generally accepted by the lay membership, and therefore deliberately not included in the budget. This hazard should not blind us to the desirability of the pastor having at his disposal an amount of money that he may use in emergencies or in delicate circumstances, with no questions asked and only a general accounting required.

If the benevolence committee feels it necessary to do so, it may define the purpose of the pastor's discretionary fund to indicate that the money may not be used for purposes otherwise budgeted for, or on items considered for the budget but rejected. In the author's opinion, the pastor's discretionary fund should be the only unparticularized account in the church financial structure. The existence of other special funds, not specifically programmed to some use, tend to defeat the concept of orderly programming and budgeting and have been known to commit the church to programs in which it did not wish to participate.

PROPERTY CONDITION AND MAINTENANCE

Property condition and maintenance is one of the most tangible items to be considered. Each year prior to the submission of its request, the church board of property planning and management should, as a matter of practice, make a thorough examination of the entire physical facility, using a checklist on which are listed the various buildings and rooms, the various utility systems, the plantings and general external appearance of the church. In the course of this annual inspection, all necessary repairs should be listed, with an indication of relative priority. Modifications or additions to the physical facility, if needed, should be carefully described and responsible estimates of costs obtained. This inspection should include a very painstaking check of the operation of doors and windows, and the condition of screens, faucets, drains, and switches. It should also include a visual inspection of the roof, gutters, and spouts, and a careful examination of the condition of paint and wallpaper, and the convenience and safety of walks and steps.

On the basis of such a detailed inspection, the submission by the property planning and management board should include two types of items: first, normal maintenance and repair, increased or decreased from previous years on the basis of the inspection; and second, a group of modifications or additions separately identified and priced for discretionary consideration. When requesting budgetary consideration for expenses involved in property maintenance and modification, the calendar period of expense should be indicated. As we shall soon see in Chapter 7, maintenance charges are particularly responsive to calendar period changes of the type often necessary in planning for the flow of cash.

PROMOTIONAL ACTIVITIES

The analysis of promotional activities should range over the entire area of public contact, to include such items of advertising and publicity as the church calendar and bulletin, church annual reports and directories, newspaper and similar advertising, and any special meetings, conventions, or conferences intended to broaden public awareness of the church's presence and purpose.

Newspaper advertising is one of the major expenses in many church budgets. In many instances, it is a predetermined expense, in that the policy of local papers quite often is to furnish a classified church directory at a fixed fee, with all churches listed expected to pay their pro rata share. Another form of advertising is that of participating with other churches in hotel and motel lobby directories. Directional signs at street intersections near the church fall in somewhat the same category. The relative benefit received from these various forms of advertising should be carefully studied. The simplest form of analysis of church advertising is for the pastor to ask new persons he meets at the worship services how they learned of the church. He thus develops an appreciation of the relative importance of the various forms of advertising. Some churches use a simple questionnaire, a small card placed in a container on the back of the church pew upon which a visitor or newcomer indicates his name, his interest, and how he learned of the church.

Another major element of promotional expense is the church's participation in special meetings, conventions, and conferences. These include events to be conducted by the local church and those at which the local church plans to be represented. There is no substitute for direct personal contact in denominational and ecumenical endeavors. If the church is to be known and appreciated for its values and efforts, it should encourage its staff and members to participate in direct contact opportunities provided at conventions and conferences. This should be a policy of the church, and should be reflected in the programming of financial assistance to its members who might attend these meetings either by designation or as volunteers.

DEBT RETIREMENT AND SERVICE

In many church budgets, the item of debt retirement and debt service dwarfs all other figures. This figure usually represents a portfolio of mortgages on church buildings, parish houses, parsonages, and camp and convention facilities. Our purpose here is not to evaluate these debt arrangements but to emphasize that, in budgeting, we must recognize debt service (the paying of interest) as a nondiscretionary item of considerable importance. It is also important to recognize debt retirement as a commendable goal toward which substantial strides should be made every year, but which is not quite as rigid a requirement as that of paying the interest.

To the extent that debt retirement and debt service constitute a tremendous drain on resources, and thereby prevent the church from accomplishing its mission, the debt should be reduced as rapidly as possible so that funds may become available for other programs. On the other hand, overly drastic efforts to retire debt have, in some cases, drawn so heavily on the resources of the church that practically all other activities were brought to a standstill. The role played by debt retirement and debt service in planning cash-flow is to be discussed in Chapter 7. In that chapter, we shall see that the choice of dates on which an interest payment is made, or on which a payment is applied to principal, can be very important.

Early in this chapter, we emphasized that the various responsible boards and committees of the church should develop their programs, determine the "price tags" relating to those programs, and conduct a comprehensive analysis prior to reporting their needs to the church programs-and-budget committee. A device successfully employed for this purpose is illustrated by Exhibits 4 and 5, taken from the *Church Program and Budgets Builder,* published by the United Church of Christ. This pamphlet is a guide to thoughtful consideration of the needs of each area of church life. Two of these program areas have been chosen as illustrative of the approach used. Exhibit 4, on page 63, pertains to provisions for public worship. Exhibit 5, on page 65, is a guide to consideration of God's house and its care. Each of these exhibits includes three sections which are explained as follows:

The first section, "We Clarify Our Purpose," attempts to define the objectives of each field of interest under consideration. We cannot overcome "routine" and have outlook and upreach in what we do until we understand our purpose and some of its fundamental implications. The committee, and such organized groups and functional services as are identified with any given area, will take time to study and discuss this section.

The second section, "We Appraise Our Present Program," seeks to ask the question, "In the light of the above objectives, what are we really accomplishing in this area?" By collective answers of "yes" or "no" to a series of questions, we hope to achieve a self-appraisal in order to mark progress. What have we been doing? Why have we been doing it? How have our activities contributed to the growth of people in their understanding of the faith, in their awareness of and commitment to Christian values, fellowship and service?

The third section, "We Plan Our Advance," calls for setting goals for the coming year and for a program required to meet those goals. A list of program suggestions is offered. The list is by no means exhaustive. The first column to the right gives opportunity to check points of active interest and possible action. The second and third columns, "Estimated Dollar Budget" and "Estimated Personnel," indicate how the approved

PUBLIC WORSHIP

I. WE CLARIFY OUR PURPOSE

When we worship in the church we prepare ourselves by centering our thoughts and emotions on God. We come together to hear the Word of God, to receive the sacraments and to offer prayer and praise to the Father, the Son and the Holy Spirit. We joyously give witness that we are a community, bound together by a common faith and a common obedience.

NOTES:

1. Christian worship is first of all a reception of what God *offers* his Church. *God Giving* and *God Speaking* is the primary mood of the scripture, the sermon, the Communion service.

2. The church is expected to *respond* as one body to what God offers — in prayers of confession, praise, thanksgiving, intercession; in hymns, offering, and communion.

3. There is an ancient, simple liturgy of offering and response which belongs to all Christian churches. It is more like a symbolic drama in which all worshipers participate than a program arranged by the minister for edification or inspiration.

4. The breaking open of the Word of God, in Scripture and sermon, and the Communion service are two high points of Reformed Protestant worship. When Communion is not celebrated, the offering (historically a part of the Communion order) remains as a reminder of all that is central in the Lord's Supper.

5. The number of worshipers may be large or small, depending upon the membership of the church, but when the number attending a service is proportionately large we are warmed and exalted by an assurance of unity and strength.

6. Plainness and directness in form, style and decorations are often more eloquent aids to worship than fussy decorations and dramatic effects. The Word of God does not need embellishment.

7. Children and young people are strongly influenced by their parents in their habits and attitudes toward public worship, especially when entire families participate in the service.

II. WE APPRAISE OUR PRESENT PROGRAM

1. Do the members understand the meaning of all portions of the service?   YES ☐   No ☐

2. Do the people feel "lifted up" and "drawn together" by their common worship? If not, why not?   YES ☐   No ☐

3. Is Holy Communion celebrated often enough? Is Baptism generally a public service in which the whole church participates?   YES ☐   No ☐

4. Is the meeting room for the service clean, beautiful, awe-inspiring?   YES ☐   No ☐

5. Is quietness maintained before the service begins, so that those who come early may be free to meditate and pray? YES ☐   No ☐

6. Are the ushers and hospitality committee alert and friendly?   YES ☐   No ☐

7. Is the friendliness of the church the real overflowing of the love of God in the hearts of the people, so no one feels that he stands alone, unwanted, unrecognized.   YES ☐   No ☐

8. Does the congregation feel a sense of participation in the service? e.g. How is the congregational singing?   YES ☐   No ☐

9. Does the choir help in leading the congregation in worship rather than seeming to perform?   YES ☐   No ☐

10. Is the music instrumental and vocal, of high order?   YES ☐   No ☐

11. Are the members of official boards faithful in attendance?   YES ☐   No ☐

12. What percentage of the members attend church regularly? What percentage of families come as Family units?   %   %

....
....
....
....

Exhibit 4.   Example of a Guide for Program Consideration—Public Worship

(Two pages from the *Church Program and Budgets Builder* published by the Stewardship Council, United Church of Christ.)

		RECOMMENDED		ESTIMATED	
III. WE PLAN OUR ADVANCE		This Year	Later	Dollar Budget	Personnel Budget
1. A commitment from each family, and each individual member of the parish to attend worship regularly					
2. Adequate financial provision for competent musical leadership and for purchase of suitable music					
3. Provision for good or new choir robes					
4. More or new hymnals of good musical and liturgical quality					
5. As large a choir as may serve advantageously					
6. To arrange if possible for junior and/or youth choirs; appoint choir mothers					
7. To teach congregation new hymns outside of worship service hours					
8. Friendly, efficient ushering procedures; to enlarge number of ushers that more men may participate on rotating basis					
9. Committee for care of flowers, candles, etc.					
10. Hospitality: couples to take turns to greet worshippers and have charge of guest book					
11. If no officer on duty, someone to direct traffic and handle parking problems					
12. An attractive literature table or rack with committee in charge					
13. To provide space, furniture, and leadership to assure small children an informal worship experience while parents attend worship; also nursery for babies					
14. Occasional study of order of worship, in light of Reformed tradition and needs of congregation					
....					
....					
....					
....					
....					
....					

Exhibit 4. Continued

GOD'S HOUSE AND ITS CARE

I. WE CLARIFY OUR PURPOSE

1. The church building is God's house and should be maintained as a building dedicated to God.
2. It is a major symbol of our faith in the community, and others will judge the Christian religion by the way we care for our church.
3. It is one of the chief tools by which we promote the encounter of God and man in worship and Christian education. It must be an efficient tool adapted to its purpose.

II. WE APPRAISE OUR PRESENT PROGRAM

1. Does our church building really testify to our highest ideals? YES ☐ No ☐
2. Do our facilities for worship inspire and encourage encounter with God? YES ☐ No ☐
3. Are we providing our children with rooms where they may best learn the gospel? YES ☐ No ☐
4. Are the windows, carvings, pictures and other objects of art in the church building and church school of the highest artistic quality and are they suitably related to the theology and teaching program of the church? YES ☐ No ☐
5. Does our building provide adequately for Christian fellowship? YES ☐ No ☐
6. Do we protect the children and adults using the church from fire and accidents? YES ☐ No ☐
7. Do we maintain proper janitorial service? YES ☐ No ☐

8. Is there a full program of inspection and maintenance of the building? YES ☐ No ☐
9. Is our church site properly landscaped and policed? Is the church a good neighbor? YES ☐ No ☐
10. Is proper parking space provided? YES ☐ No ☐
11. Does the church have a suitable parsonage adequately maintained? YES ☐ No ☐
12. Does the church carry adequate insurance against loss by fire, windstorm, boiler explosion or aircraft damage? Does it carry liability insurance including complete coverage of medical expenses for persons injured? Has a new insurance appraisal been made within the last three years? YES ☐ No ☐

....

....

....

....

Exhibit 5. Example of a Guide for Program Consideration— God's House and Its Care

(Two pages from the *Church Program and Budgets Builder* published by the Stewardship Council, United Church of Christ.)

		RECOMMENDED		ESTIMATED	
III. WE PLAN OUR ADVANCE		This Year	Later	Dollar Budget	Personnel Budget
1. To create a study committee to read books and study the facilities of the church to see how well the building qualifies as a tool and symbol of our faith					
2. Formation of a church art committee to study religious art and to help improve the art program of the church					
3. To have a complete fire and safety check of the building, covering the following and other items: Adequate exits Exit doors — easily opened Staircases — safe Hallways — lighted Furnace room — fire-proof door kept closed Property clear of inflammable materials Wiring — good condition Furnaces, stoves and other appliances — good condition Sidewalks — smooth and free of ice Stair-rails Fire drills — regular					
4. To have trustees make complete annual inspection of the church building and parsonage as to their physical condition and maintenance					
5. Adoption of a long-term schedule for maintenance and future property improvements					
6. To form working committees to a assist in proper maintenance of the building and care of the church site, landscaping, flowers and lawn.					
....					
....					
....					
....					
....					

Exhibit 5.   Continued

projects and emphases may ultimately become part of the budget.

As the expressed needs of the church are assembled by the programs-and-budget committee, the various items, many of which have been described above, are entered into the expenditure worksheet. The details of this procedure will be considered in Chapter 5.

STUDY OF THE OPERATING PERIOD

In addition to the specific study of the many significant areas of need, an examination must also be made of how these needs were stated and met in past and current operating periods. This should be based on material maintained by the church treasurer and the financial secretary. Against each item should be charted the amount requested in previous periods and the variance experienced, either under or over the amount budgeted. This procedure serves several purposes. In one sense, it is a way of measuring the capability of the various church activities to estimate their needs, thus providing a basis for determining assistance they might need in their current budgetary effort. More important, this study of the operating period identifies areas in which the church is failing to accomplish its program, and, therefore, not using all the funds planned. Before arbitrarily deciding that a request was too high, an investigation should be conducted to determine the reasons for failure to accomplish something which at one time had been thought to be very important.

Those cases where funds used during the operating period exceeded what was budgeted might indicate that the original estimates were not as carefully made as they might have been. The possibility always exists that unforeseen changes in price, or other matters beyond control, were responsible.

HOPE LUTHERAN CHURCH
ST. LOUIS, MISSOURI

EIGHT YEAR COMPARISON OF TOTAL EXPENDITURES
ANALYZED IN TERMS OF PERCENTAGE OF TOTAL INCOME AND AMOUNT PER COMMUNICANT
DECEMBER 31, 1961

		(1)	(2)	(3)	(4)	(5)	(6)	(7)	(8)
FISCAL YEAR	COMMUNICANT MEMBERS	PASTORAL SERVICE	CHRISTIAN EDUCATION	ADMINISTRATIVE AND GENERAL	RETIREMENT OF CAPITAL DEBT	TOTAL CURRENT OPERATIONS	WORLD MISSIONS	LUTHERAN HIGH SCHOOL OPERATIONS	LUTHERAN HIGH SCHOOL DEBT RETIREMENT

AMOUNT

FISCAL YEAR	PASTORAL SERVICE	CHRISTIAN EDUCATION	ADMINISTRATIVE AND GENERAL	RETIREMENT OF CAPITAL DEBT	TOTAL CURRENT OPERATIONS	WORLD MISSIONS	LUTHERAN HIGH SCHOOL OPERATIONS	LUTHERAN HIGH SCHOOL DEBT RETIREMENT
1954	$ 24 000	$ 26 204	$ 6 700	$ 43 565	$ 100 469	$ 15 162	$ 3 600	$ 374
1955	25 316	28 832	6 622	42 015	102 785	18 164	3 600	5 655
1956	33 236	29 966	6 415	41 294	110 911	14 382	4 245	16 598
1957	32 985	30 486	4 576	25 861	93 908	18 513	5 314	15 332
1958	33 034	39 080	6 703	11 121	89 938	24 116	7 193	14 508
1959	34 764	40 425	6 276	5 000	86 465	26 772	7 653	8 009
1960	33 205	45 363	6 463	9 086	94 117	29 983	8 959	1 792
1961	32 251	48 489	5 864	5 585	92 189	31 767	9 148	1 830
TOTALS	$ 248 791	$ 288 845	$ 49 619	$ 183 527	$ 770 782	$ 178 859	$ 49 712	$ 64 098

PERCENT OF INCOME

FISCAL YEAR	PASTORAL SERVICE	CHRISTIAN EDUCATION	ADMINISTRATIVE AND GENERAL	RETIREMENT OF CAPITAL DEBT	TOTAL CURRENT OPERATIONS	WORLD MISSIONS	LUTHERAN HIGH SCHOOL OPERATIONS	LUTHERAN HIGH SCHOOL DEBT RETIREMENT
1954	19.9%	21.7%	5.5%	36.0%	83.1%	12.6%	3.0%	.3%
1955	18.9	21.6	4.9	31.4	76.8	13.6	2.7	4.2
1956	22.6	20.3	4.4	28.0	75.3	9.8	2.9	11.3
1957	23.7	21.9	3.3	18.6	67.5	13.3	3.8	11.0
1958	22.5	26.6	4.6	7.6	61.3	16.4	4.9	9.9
1959	24.0	27.9	4.3	3.4	59.6	18.5	5.3	5.5
1960	22.4	30.5	4.4	6.1	63.4	20.2	6.0	1.2
1961	20.4	30.6	3.7	3.5	58.2	20.0	5.7	1.2
AVERAGE	21.8%	25.3%	4.4%	16.1%	67.6%	15.7%	4.4%	5.6%

AMOUNT PER COMMUNICANT

FISCAL YEAR	PASTORAL SERVICE	CHRISTIAN EDUCATION	ADMINISTRATIVE AND GENERAL	RETIREMENT OF CAPITAL DEBT	TOTAL CURRENT OPERATIONS	WORLD MISSIONS	LUTHERAN HIGH SCHOOL OPERATIONS	LUTHERAN HIGH SCHOOL DEBT RETIREMENT
1954 (1,404)	$ 17 10	$ 18 65	$ 4 80	$ 31 00	$ 71 55	$ 10 85	$ 2 55	$ 25
1955 (1,431)	17 70	20 15	4 65	29 35	71 85	12 70	2 50	3 95
1956 (1,501)	22 15	20 00	4 25	27 50	.73 90	9 60	2 80	11 05
1957 (1,424)	23 20	21 40	3 20	18 15	65 95	13 00	3 75	10 75
1958 (1,503)	22 00	26 00	4 45	7 40	59 85	16 05	4 80	9 65
1959 (1,470)	23 65	27 50	4 25	3 40	58 80	18 20	5 20	5 45
1960 (1,481)	22 40	30 65	4 35	6 15	63 55	20 25	6 05	1 20
1961 (1,491)	21 65	32 50	3 90	3 75	61 80	21 30	6 15	1 20
AVERAGE (1,463)	$ 21 25	$ 24 70	$ 4 25	$ 15 65	$ 65 85	$ 15 30	$ 4 25	$ 5 45

Exhibit 6. Example of a Detailed Analysis of Church Expenditures

(Furnished by Hope Lutheran Church, St. Louis, Missouri.)

| | (9) LUTHERAN HOSPITAL BUILDING FUND | (10) LUTH. CHARIT. COUNCIL OF CHURCHES | (11) OTHER AGENCIES AND CHARITIES | (12) TOTAL MISSIONS AND CHARITIES | (13) TOTAL EXPENDITURES | (14) ADDITIONS TO FUND BALANCES LOCAL AND AREA EXPANSION | (15) CURRENT FUND SURPLUS |
FISCAL YEAR							
			AMOUNT				
1954	$ 1 480	$ 2 500	$ 644	$ 23 760	$ 124 229	$ -0-	$ (3 419)
1955	1 887	2 713	1 558	33 577	136 362	-0-	(2 497)
1956	1 140	2 936	1 675	40 976	151 887	-0-	(4 552)
1957	680	3 026	1 837	44 702	138 610	-0-	399
1958	1 006	3 773	723	51 319	141 257	-0-	5 389
1959	5 301	3 608	2 590	53 933	140 398	-0-	4 686
1960	4 063	4 568	485	49 850	143 967	3 047	1 478
1961	4 118	4 971	1 293	53 127	145 316	10 451	2 765
TOTALS	$ 19 675	$ 28 095	$ 10 805	$ 351 244	$1 122 026	$ 13 498	$ 4 249
			PERCENT OF INCOME				
1954	1.2%	2.1%	.5%	19.7%	102.8%	-0-%	(2.8%)
1955	1.4	2.0	1.2	25.1	101.9	-0-	(1.9)
1956	.7	2.0	1.1	27.8	103.1	-0-	(3.1)
1957	.5	2.2	1.4	32.2	99.7	-0-	.3
1958	.7	2.6	.5	35.0	96.3	-0-	3.7
1959	3.6	2.5	1.8	37.2	96.8	-0-	3.2
1960	2.7	3.1	.4	33.6	97.0	2.0	1.0
1961	2.6	3.2	.8	33.5	91.7	6.6	1.7
AVERAGE	1.7%	2.5%	.9%	30.8%	98.4%	1.2%	.4%
			AMOUNT PER COMMUNICANT				
1954	$ 1 05	$ 1 80	$ 45	$ 16 95	$ 88 50	$ -0-	$ (2 45)
1955	1 30	1 90	1 10	23 45	95 30	-0-	(1 75)
1956	75	2 00	1 10	27 30	101 20	-0-	(3 05)
1957	50	2 10	1 30	31 40	97 35	-0-	25
1958	65	2 50	50	34 15	94 00	-0-	3 55
1959	3 60	2 45	1 80	36 70	95 50	-0-	3 20
1960	2 75	3 10	30	33 65	97 20	2 05	1 00
1961	2 75	3 35	90	35 65	97 45	7 00	1 85
AVERAGE	$ 1 70	$ 2 40	$ 90	$ 30 00	$ 95 85	$ 1 15	$ 40

Exhibit 6. Continued

The point of view most useful to the programs-and-budget committee is that an overestimate in one area, if it is allowed to stand, will be perpetuated, acting to prevent inclusion in the budget of some other worthy activity. For this reason, items that fall short in actual expenditure of the amounts budgeted should be examined with great care.

The analysis of expenditures should be accomplished in a degree of detail appropriate to the local situation. An example of a very thorough analysis is shown in Exhibit 6, on page 68. This exhibit comes from the annual audit report of Hope Lutheran Church, St. Louis, Missouri. The Hope Lutheran Church adds to its detailed analysis a very meaningful graphic presentation, shown at Exhibit 7, on page 71.

It is important to reiterate here a point made earlier. Successful budgeting is not measured by the closeness with which estimates are met, but rather by the programs accomplished, regardless of how accurately they were budgeted.

REALISM AND OBJECTIVITY

Examination of the needs of the church must be conducted objectively. As individuals accustomed to the life and the ways of the church, we usually try not to be critical and suspicious. However, when working on church programs and budget, we must be realistic enough to recognize that it is human nature to overstate requirements, either in enthusiasm over what is being planned or in a deliberate effort to build a defense against reductions of the amount requested.

In church budgeting, one should certainly hope that various requirements are openly stated, that nothing is hidden or misrepresented, and that requests are not deliberately "padded" against the possibility of cuts by the programs-and-budget committee or the board of finance. Only with experience gained in the local church, and through wide acquaintance with the programs of the church and the peo

HOPE LUTHERAN CHURCH
ST. LOUIS, MISSOURI
EIGHT YEAR GRAPHIC COMPARISON OF OPERATIONS
DECEMBER 31, 1961

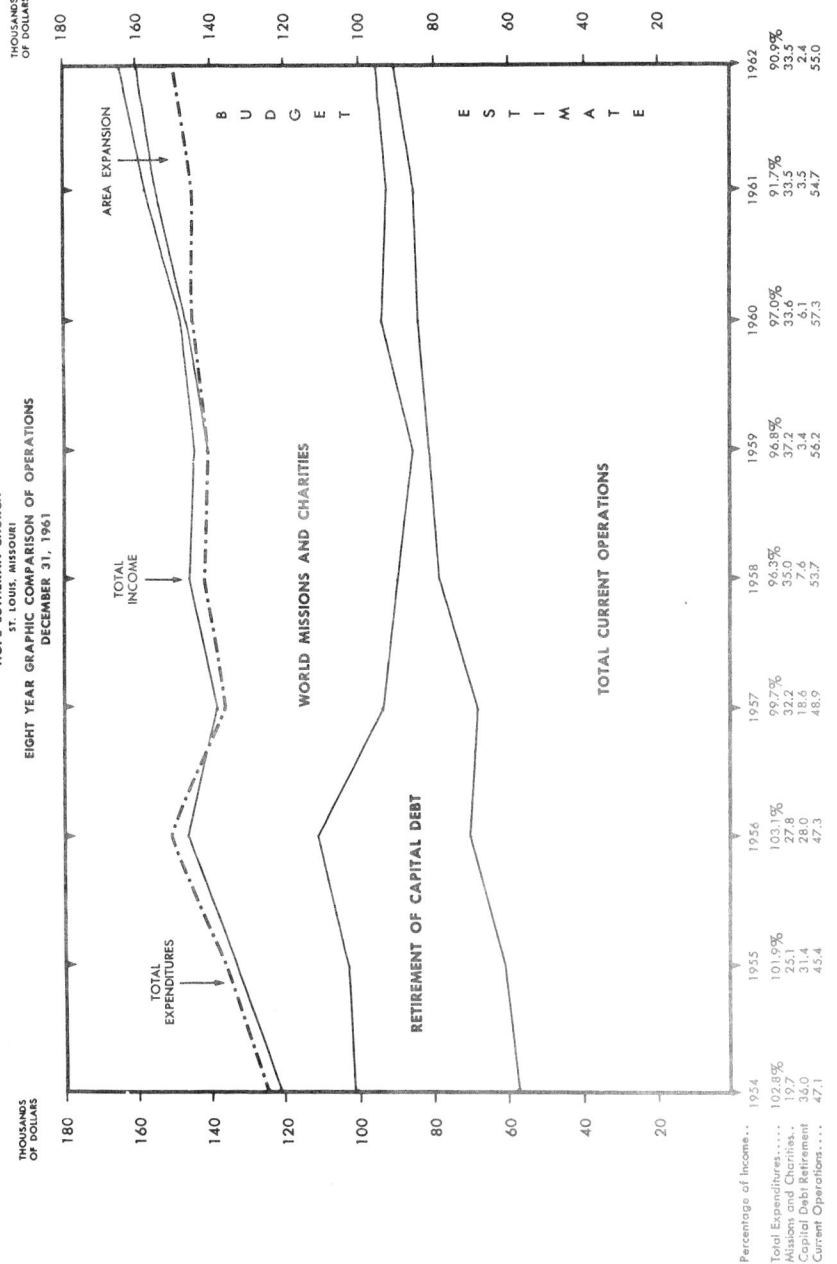

Percentage of Income...	1954	1955	1956	1957	1958	1959	1960	1961	1962
Total Expenditures.....	102.8%	101.9%	103.1%	99.7%	96.3%	96.8%	97.0%	91.7%	90.9%
Missions and Charities..	19.7	25.1	27.8	32.2	35.0	37.2	33.6	33.5	33.5
Capital Debt Retirement	36.0	31.4	28.0	18.6	7.6	3.4	6.1	3.5	2.4
Current Operations....	47.1	45.4	47.3	48.9	53.7	56.2	57.3	54.7	55.0

ple responsible for them, can we be sure that the assembled statement of needs is realistic and objective.

In the next chapter, we shall continue our identification and analysis of individual items, turning our attention to items of income. How can we best project the revenue of our church? What are some useful criteria of individual giving? What other sources of income should be budgeted?

Chapter 4

IDENTIFYING AND ANALYZING FINANCIAL RESOURCES OF CHURCHES

Now THAT WE have given preliminary consideration to the financial needs of the church, let us turn to the financial resources of the church.

A surprisingly large number of individual church budgets do not identify sources of expected income. Such budgets are only "half budgets." We must carefully examine the sources of church income, and we must keep the membership informed not only of these sources, but also of the reliance placed on each. This is the beginning of our unified plan of receipts. Without careful study of receipts, it is impossible to set realistic programs and goals. There must be a conviction on the part of the programs-and-budget committee that the church is realizing its full resources before that committee acts to definitize its programs.

Members of the church should be kept informed as to sources of financial support. The average person is more inclined to contribute when he realizes the relative importance of his contribution, not only as it compares with the contributions of other persons, but also as it relates to amounts realized from other sources. Some would urge that too much disclosure of the amounts pledged creates a bad effect, because individual contributors will try to determine a *pro rata* share and will reduce their pledges to that share.

People who might take this approach could do so regardless of whether the various sources of church income are itemized in the budget.

The complexity of items entering into the receipts section of the church budget can be appreciated from the following list:

Pledges or dues

Plate offerings

Gifts and bequests

Endowments and memorials

Contributions for use of facilities

Special events and drives

Cemetery charges

Sale of Bibles, books, tracts

Income from trust funds and investments

Interest on bank deposits

As estimates of the resources of the church are assembled by the programs-and-budget committee, the various items are entered into the resources (income) worksheet. Details of this procedure will be considered in Chapter 5.

PLEDGES OR DUES

The largest single source of revenue or income for the typical church is derived from the pledges of individual members and family units. These pledges are recorded in many ways. Most churches periodically conduct a formal drive to secure written pledges. Others publish a schedule of dues or fees that each family or individual is expected to remit. Still other churches work on what is known as an "open-end pledge," under which the pledge, once made, is considered as continuing year after year until the pledging member, through his own volition, changes the amount.

Our purpose here is not to examine the techniques and problems of church fund raising. That is the subject of another book in this series, *Church Fund Raising*, by George W. Harrison. Our purpose is to make sure that the budget we prepare includes realistic estimates of funds to be raised from all the many sources. Also, our planning in regard to income, the receipts portion of our budget, is a key element of the fund-raising effort. It establishes the target for that effort, and the yardstick by which success in that effort is to be judged.

The budgetary process produces another document of great importance from the fund-raising point of view, the appeal budget. We shall return to the role of the appeal budget in Chapter 6.

In making estimates of individual or family-unit pledges, we find that a useful approach is through community per capita income, using as sources Federal and local government publications and studies conducted by several of the business and financial magazines. Having determined the income pattern for the church community, we can project what revenue might be realized from the membership at various levels of commitment: the Biblical tithing figure of 10 per cent, at 5 per cent, 3 per cent, or even at 1 per cent. The figure determined in this way should be contrasted with the "giving experience" of the local church. The figure developed from the income statistics represents a "possible revenue," and the "giving experience" figure represents a previously attained revenue. A figure falling between the two would be most useful in setting fund-raising goals and in initial budgeting.

An excellent illustration of the use of these techniques is provided by the Stewardship Services of the Southern Baptist Convention. (See Exhibit 8, page 76.) The Southern Baptist Convention also furnishes an aid for use in analyzing the giving record of the church. It is shown as Exhibit 9, page 79.

This We Are Able

A Study of the Giving Potential of the Church

You doubtless would like to see your church accomplish many things which hitherto have seemed impossible. But before trying to reach some of those goals, just what is the true potential of your congregation?

I. The Use of This Workbook

1. This is the second of three workbooks to be completed by the budget planning committee in drawing up a proposed budget for the coming year. The workbook, "This Is the Record," (FB-2), should be completed before starting on this one.

2. Churches with large budget planning committees may divide into subcommittees, with one subcommittee working on "This Is the Record," while the other works simultaneously on "This We Are Able." The entire committee will want to work together on the third workbook, "This We Propose" (FB-4).

II. Lifting Our Sights

1. The study of "This Is the Record" has shown the present giving habits of the congregation. Should next year's budget goal be set merely on past records? Actually, is not the main question, What is the congregation able to do, rather than, What has it been doing?

2. This workbook, "This We Are Able," is designed to do just that. It enables the committee to determine just what the giving potential of the congregation actually is. Thus, the committee can suggest a budget goal more in keeping with the church's capabilities rather than its past record.

III. The Basis of True Potentiality

1. But how is the committee to determine what the congregation is able to give? Is such to be based merely on personal opinion?

2. At this point, we turn to the Scriptures. The Bible teaches the tithe as a minimum. It was commanded in the Old Testament. It was commended by Jesus. And Christians who

are tithers testify to the satisfactions of tith ing and to the fact that God does fulfill h promise and "pours out a blessing." T spiritual blessings are more important, th bear witness.

3. What could your church do if every memb were a tither? What budget could it rais What buildings could it erect? What bran Sunday schools could it sponsor? How mu more could it give to world missions throu the Cooperative Program?

4. Should not, then, next year's budget goal l commensurate with the tithe potential your entire membership?

5. This would not mean that the budget go should equal the tithe potential. The tith potential shows what could be done if eve member had the proper interest. But sin the average Southern Baptist church nc gives only about one-third of the tithe, would be highly ambitious to think the enti tithe could be reached in one effort.

6. Somewhere between what the church h been doing ("This Is the Record") and wh the church could be doing ("This We A Able") will fall the budget goal for next yea The budget planning committee will recon mend such a goal—one that is challengir enough to appeal to the imagination, y realistic enough to be achieved.

IV. How Determine the Tithe Potential

1. This workbook suggests three ways to arriv at the tithe potential in your church. Stuc the three ways, and select the one whic will be most accurate for your communit; Or, you may wish to use all three method and then take an average of the three.

2. The methods suggested on the followir pages include using the previous record c known tithers in your congregation, the pe capita income of individuals in your state or the effective buying power of individua: in your community.

Exhibit 8.   Worksheet for Studying the Giving Potential of a Church

(Prepared by SBC Stewardship Services.)

Plan A: Determining the Tithe Potential on Basis of Giving Record

Assuming that the present tithers in your church represent a cross section of the income of all the membership, add together the total contributions of all the tithers in your church for the first six months of this year. Then double this amount to arrive at an estimate of their total annual contributions. Next, divide the total contributions of all tithers by the number of tithers. This will show the average annual contribution made by tithers in your congregation. To find the tithe potential of the entire congregation, multiply the total number of church members by the average tither's contribution.

In making this computation, it will be necessary to check the individual record of contributions of the tithers. Make certain to include children who are tithers to get a cross-section of financial ability. If individual records have not been maintained, this method could not be used unless there were some other source of information concerning the average contribution of all the tithers.

Formula for arriving at tithe potential through Plan A:

a. Total resident membership of our church: _____

b. Total number of tithers in our church, for whom we have giving records: _____

c. Total contributions of above tithers for first *six months* of this year: $_____

d. Multiply the amount in line c. by two and enter here: _____
   (This shows estimate of total contributions of tithers for a one-year period.)

e. Divide the amount in line d. by the number in line b. and enter the result here: $_____
   (This shows the average per capita gift of tithers in your church.)

f. Multiply the amount in line e. by the number in line a. and enter here: $_____
   (This shows the potential income of your church for next year if every member were a tither.)

Plan B: Determining the Tithe Potential on Basis of Per Capita Income

A second method of determining the tithe potential is to secure the annual per capita income of residents of your state, multiply that by the number of members in the church, and take one-tenth of that amount.

Each year, the July-August-September issue of the *Quarterly Review* shows the per capita income of each state. (The *Quarterly Review* may be ordered from the Baptist Sunday School Board, 127 Ninth Avenue, North, Nashville, Tennessee.) In the table of contents, look under "Income, per capita personal." Turn then to the appropriate page, and you will find the annual per capita income for your state.

Before you can use your state's per capita income figure for your congregation, it may require some adjustment. Remember these are average figures and may represent extremes of income not represented in your church. If so, you will need to adjust the per capita figure upward accordingly.

Too, the per capita figures include infants and small children. Since Baptist churches do not include these in their membership, the per capita income of their members would be correspondingly higher than the average per capita. Census figures indicate that each per capita figure needs to be multiplied by one and one fourth to arrive at a usable figure for dealing with church memberships not including smaller children.

Formula for arriving at tithe potential through Plan B:

a. Enter here number of resident church members: _____

b. Enter here, from the *Quarterly Review* or other source, the latest per capita income figure for your state: $_____

c. Multiply line a. by line b. and enter the result here: $_____

d. To adjust for the absence of infants and small children, multiply line c. by one and one fourth and enter the result here: $_____
   (This shows the total annual income of your church membership.)

e. Take one tenth of the amount in line d. and enter here: $_____
   (This shows the annual tithe potential of your church. That is, this is the potential income of your church for next year if every member were a tither.)

Exhibit 8. Continued

Plan C: Determining the Tithe Potential on Basis of Per Capita Effective Buying Income

If you wish to secure a more accurate income picture for your town, city, or county, you will want to secure the per capita effective buying income figures for your county. These figures will, of course, be more accurate than the per capita income for your state. Since financial conditions vary so much from county to county even within a single state, statistics dealing with your specific county may be more helpful for your church.

"Per capita effective buying income" means the income each person in your county has available for spending *after* federal and state income taxes have been deducted. Each year, the May 10 issue of *Sales Management* magazine shows the per capita effective buying income of every county and approximately 1,700 cities in the United States. This issue is available in many public and educational libraries. Or it may be purchased at $4.00 per copy (Sales Management Magazine, 386 Fourth Avenue, New York 16, New York). Several statistics are given for each county, but make sure to use the *per capita effective buying income* (rather than per family income).

These figures will be used much like the per capita figures in Plan B, with one exception. The figure must be revised upwards to include the approximately 20 per cent which has been deducted for federal and state income taxes. That is, the figures in *Sales Management* represent about 80 per cent of the total per capita income.

Formula for arriving at tithe potential through Plan C:

a. Enter here number of resident church members: _____

b. Copy here from May 10 issue of *Sales Management* magazine the per capita effective buying income for your city or county: $_____

c. Multiply line a. by line b. and enter the result here: $_____

d. To adjust for the absence of infants and small children, multiply line c. by one and one fourth and enter the result here: $_____

e. Divide the amount in line d. by eight, and enter the result here: $_____
(The figure eight is used as a divider instead of ten to show the tithe before taxes. The amount now shown in line e. is the annual tithe potential income of your church for next year if every member were a tither.)

FB-3
SBC Stewardship Services
127 Ninth Avenue, North
Nashville 3, Tennessee

Exhibit 8. Continued

This Is The Record

An Analysis of the Giving Record of the Church

"A study of our record opened our eyes," reported a businessman who is a deacon in his church. "We had never made an analysis of what our members are doing. We were rather pleased with our record. But this study made us realize we were barely touching our possibilities. The first result was agreement that we ought to double our present budget. The second result was that we did."

I. The Value of a Giving Record

1. This is the first of three workbooks used by the budget planning committee. The other two are "This We Are Able" (FB-3) and "This We Propose" (FB-4). With this first workbook, the committee analyzes the giving records of the Sunday school and church membership.

2. Before the budget planning committee proposes a new budget goal for the coming year, it is vital to know how well the members have been giving the previous year. This workbook will answer such questions as, How many tithers in our church? How many who make annual pledges? What are the per capita, modal, and median gifts of our members? How does the giving of tithers compare with non-tithers? Of pledgers with non-pledgers? How many are giving little or nothing? Is a small percentage of the membership carrying a disproportionate share of the budget? On the basis of the percentage of our total budget going to world missions through the Cooperative Program, how rapidly is that percentage growing?

II. How to Secure This Information

1. Remember, first, that although the committee deals with the giving records of individual members, publicity is never given as to which person gave what amount. You will present a total giving picture—not one of specific members. Committee members who compile this information will not discuss outside the committee the giving record of individual members by name.

2. The committee will need these resource materials for completing this workbook:

    (1) Individual giving records for each church member (regardless of age), and for each Sunday school member who is not a church member (regardless of age). If individual records have not been kept, the committee cannot complete this workbook. Valuable information will consequently be unobtainable. Start now keeping individual records of contributions so you can profit from this workbook next year. Use Form 495-21991, Record of Contributions, available at Baptist book stores.

    (2) All pledge cards signed during last year's budget campaign.

    (3) Church treasurer's records for the current year.

III. How to Complete the Analysis Worksheets

1. Worksheets for analyzing the church and Sunday school members' records begin on the next page. Note there are eleven columns, nine of which are blank and to be filled in by the committee.

2. The first step is to secure the individual giving records of each church and Sunday school member for the current year. Since most committees will use this workbook in late summer or fall, it will not be possible to get each member's giving total for the entire year. The simplest way is to total what each member has given for the first six months of this year, January through June. When "Mr. and Mrs." have joint pledge, count each as giving one half the total.

3. After each member's giving record has been totaled for January through June, the committee is ready to tabulate. Use check and double check procedure for this computation as in $\cancel{||||}$ II. That is, one check mark is entered either in column three, four, five, six, seven, eight, nine, or ten. But no mark is made in more than one column for any one member.

4. Assume that the first member to be tabulated is Joe Avis, and that during the first six months of this year he gave $135.00. Find this amount in column one. Next, compare it with the figure opposite it in column two, which will show that his giving falls between $5.01 and $5.50 per week. Now determine in which of the eight columns a check is to be made for Mr. Avis. If he is a church member, and 28 years of age, and made a pledge last year, enter his check mark in the first blank column opposite "5.01 - 5.50." If he, for example, is not a church member, is 16 years old, and did not make a pledge last year, his check mark goes in the eighth blank column. Since there are eight possible categories under which any one member might be checked, the committee should set aside the necessary time to do this carefully and methodically.

5. Note that the "six-month total" in column one is for convenience in computation only. The "per week" amount is always used for promotional and publicity purposes.

IV. Why This Study?

1. In many churches, the committee will be surprised at the results of this study. In a few, they may be shocked as it becomes apparent how few of the members are carrying the major financial responsibility.

2. The picture gained will be shared with the congregation, particularly through the campaign newspapers, the Sunday bulletin, pulpit announcements, etc.

Exhibit 9.   Worksheet for Analyzing the Giving Record of a Church

(Prepared by SBC Stewardship Services.)

WORKSHEET FOR ANALYSIS OF THE GIVING RECORD OF _____

COMPUTED ON THE BASIS

TOTAL Gifts for Six-Month Period	Avg. Amount Per Week	CHURCH MEMBERS			
		Pledging		Not Pledging	
		Adults and Y. P.	Under 17	Adults and Y. P.	Under 17
Nothing	Nothing				
.01- .25	Less Than .01				
.26- 13.00	.01- .50				
13.01- 26.00	.51- 1.00				
26.00- 39.00	1.01- 1.50				
39.01- 52.00	1.51- 2.00				
52.01- 65.00	2.01- 2.50				
65.01- 78.00	2.51- 3.00				

403.01- 416.00	15.51-16.00				
416.01- 429.00	16.01-16.50				
429.01- 442.00	16.51-17.00				
442.01- 455.00	17.01-17.50				
455.01- 468.00	17.51-18.00				
468.01- 481.00	18.01-18.50				
481.01- 494.00	18.51-19.00				
494.01- 507.00	19.01-19.50				
507.01- 520.00	19.51-20.00				
520.01- 650.00	20.01-25.00				
650.01- 780.00	25.01-30.00				
780.01- 910.00	30.01-35.00				
910.01-1040.00	35.01-40.00				
1040.01-1170.00	40.01-45.00				
1170.01-1300.00	45.01-50.00				
	Above $50.00				

Exhibit 9.   Continued

CH, FOR THE SIX-MONTH PERIOD _____ THROUGH _____ , 19 ___

TAL GIFTS THROUGH THE CHURCH TREASURY

NON-CHURCH MEMBERS IN SUNDAY SCHOOL				TOTAL
Pledging		Not Pledging		
ults and Y. P.	Under 17	Adults and Y. P.	Under 17	

Exhibit 9. Continued

SUMMARY OF THE GIVING RECORD OF _____ _____ BAPTIST CHURCH

1. Number of resident church members: .... _____

2. Number of Sunday school pupils not church members: .... _____

3. Total of both church and S.S. members: .... _____

4. Number who made pledges in last year's budget campaign (both church and S.S. members): ... _____

5. Number failing to make pledges (both church and S.S. members): .... _____

6. Of those who made pledges last year, how many signed to tithe? .... _____

7. What is the total number of church and S.S. members not reported as tithers? .... _____

8. What were the total budget receipts of the church for the first six months of this year? ....$_____

9. What was the weekly per capita gift of all church and Sunday school members for the first six months of this year? (Divide line three into line eight. Then divide that amount by 26 to get this weekly figure.) ....$_____

10. What was the total amount given to world missions through the Cooperative Program the first six months of this year? ....$_____

11. What was the percentage of the total budget given through the Cooperative Program the first six months of this year? (Divide line eight into line ten.) .... _____

12. What was the weekly MODAL gift of the church and Sunday school members the first six months of this year? Refer back to the worksheets on preceding pages. After totals have been entered in the last column—column eleven—look in that column to find the largest figure. Then refer back to column two and find the weekly amount given by that number of persons (e.g., $2.01-2.50). This amount in column two is the MODAL gift, that is, the one amount given by more contributors than any other single amount. (You may wish to show two modal gifts. First, the one single amount given by the largest number of those who made some contribution during the six-month period. Second, the one single amount given by the largest number of members including both those who gave something and those who gave nothing. The point here is that the second modal gift figure may show that more members gave *nothing* than any other single amount.) Enter here the modal gift of your congregation: ....$_____

13. What was the MEDIAN gift of the church and Sunday school members during the first six months of this year? Again refer back to the worksheets on preceding pages. The MEDIAN gift means that half of the members give more than that amount, half less than that amount. It is *not* the *average* gift. To find the MEDIAN gift, get a grand total of figures in the last column of all the worksheets. Take one half of that total. Then count from the bottom of the last column until the figure is reached which represents one half of the total. For example, if there are 250 individuals whose record is tabulated on the worksheets, one half of that is 125. Read up the last column, adding the figures until you reach, for example, 125. When you reach that point, refer to column two on the same line, "Amount per week." The median of giving is the amount in that column, e.g., $5.00 to $5.50. One half the members give more than this amount, one half give less. Enter here that amount which is the median gift for your congregation: ....$_____

14. Refer back to the worksheets. Where is the heaviest concentration of liberal givers—among those who pledged, or those not making pledges? What does this show about the importance of leading members to give? Do the records substantiate the frequent excuse, "I do not believe in pledging, but I will give anyway?" Or, do they indicate that the persons who pledge are ordinarily the ones who do the significant giving? What would happen if we could double the number of pledgers as many churches have done with the use of this Program?

FB-2

SBC Stewardship Services

127 Ninth Avenue, North

Nashville, Tennessee

Exhibit 9. Continued

Still another step in the analysis of giving is to compare your church with the national average for your denomination. This information is published periodically by the National Council of Churches of Christ in the United States of America, 475 Riverside Drive, New York 27, N.Y. For various fiscal periods ending in 1960 and 1961 this report summarized giving per member over 13 years of age as shown below.

AVERAGE ANNUAL PER-MEMBER GIVING
FOR ALL PURPOSES

Reformed Church in America	$104.53
Presbyterian Church in the U.S.	101.44
United Presbyterian Church in the U.S.A.	84.31
American Evangelical Lutheran Church	83.63
Moravian Church, Northern Province	82.95
Augustana Evangelical Lutheran Church	80.88
Evangelical and Reformed Church	76.58
Congregational Christian Churches	73.20
United Lutheran Church in America	70.86
Church of the Brethren	68.33
Evangelical United Brethren Church	65.28
Protestant Episcopal Church	64.51
Christian Churches (Disciples of Christ)	63.26
The Methodist Church	55.14
Unity of the Brethren	54.48
Seventh Day Baptist General Conference	50.35
American Baptist Convention	48.06

A very resourceful way of estimating giving potential is suggested by the Commission on Stewardship of the Lutheran Church in America. A simple mimeographed card, known as the "Capacity Calculator," is used.

THE CAPACITY CALCULATOR

A. 0	0,	0	⓪	⓪.	B. 0	0,	0	0	⓪.
9	9,	9	9	9.	9	9,	9	9	9.
8	⑧,	8	8	8.	8	8,	⑧	8	8.
7	7,	7	7	7.	7	⑦,	7	7	7.
6	6,	6	6	6.	6	6,	6	6	6.
5	5,	⑤	5	5.	5	5,	5	⑤	5.
4	4,	4	4	4.	4	4,	4	4	4.
3	3,	3	3	3.	3	3,	3	3	3.
2	2,	2	2	2.	2	2,	2	2	2.
1	1,	1	1	1.	1	1,	1	1	1.
	Ⓨⓡ. Mo. Wk.					Ⓨⓡ. Mo. Wk.			

The purpose is to get some idea of the congregation's ability to support the program of the church. At a meeting of the membership, the cards are distributed with the explanation that this is an attempt to estimate giving potential. There is no need for members to sign their names; the completed cards are simply dropped into a box. Using Part A, the members are asked to circle (as has been done here) the numbers each considers to be the average family income in the parish. This may be estimated on a yearly, monthly, or weekly basis. For the wage earner, this would probably mean "take home pay"; for the farmer and any other individual in business for himself, the "adjusted gross income." The meeting leader might help things along by saying, "Families in our congregation are average for the community. They are all probably making somewhere between $2,000 and $10,000 a year. What do you think an average might be?"

After each person has had time to circle the numbers indicating his idea of average income, he is asked to indicate in Part B his own income. The Commission on Stewardship advises, "Don't quibble about taxes or anything else. Just ask them to help by circling in Part B the figures that apply to their situation."

After all the "capacity calculator" cards are collected, the programs-and-budget committee averages all the Part A entries, then averages all the Part B entries, and strikes an average of the two. A more refined (weighted average) approach could, of course, be employed if desired. Hopefully, 10 per cent of this figure would give at least a "point-of-departure" estimate of giving per family to be used in further deliberations of the programs-and-budget committee.

In Reform Hebrew congregations, the pledge of financial support frequently takes the form of a voluntary subscription based on a graduated dues schedule. A typical dues schedule serves our purpose here as still another way of establishing an estimate of income for use in budget development. For example, in 1959 the dues brackets of Temple Isaiah, of Los Angeles, California, were:

Income	Dues
Up to $7,500 per annum	$125 — 150
$7,500 to $15,000	$150 — 200 — 250
$15,000 to $20,000	$250 — 300 — 350
$20,000 to $25,000	$350 — 400 — 450
$25,000 and over	$450 and above

As the program budget cycle proceeds, pledges should be recorded as "in hand" or "late." In church finance, the door should always be left open for late receipts. The budget should recognize such receipts and include estimated amounts covering them.

Our study of pledge income should not stop with the membership of the church. It should include nonmembers —perhaps more appropriately called "friends." Many churches overlook the potential giving of individuals who find some obstacle to formal membership in the church but who, at the same time, are willing to add to its financial support. Certainly this must be recognized in fund raising and in budgetary action.

The younger members of the church family should also be encouraged to provide their share of support for church programs. This is a somewhat controversial matter, but certainly there is valid argument that the habit and responsibility of pledging to the church should be begun at an early age. Therefore, children and young adults should be given the opportunity to commit themselves to a modest level of financial support to the church.

Experienced churchmen realize that, with the passing of time and the changing of circumstances, certain pledges or subscriptions become uncollectible. It is unrealistic not to anticipate this factor in church budgeting. Having determined a gross amount that the church expects will be pledged, an experience-developed percentage should be applied to reduce this amount to a net total. Should the papers relating to the church budget openly indicate that noncollection of some pledges is anticipated? This procedure seems both realistic and honest and is, therefore, recommended.

In the church operating on a unified budget, to which all participants contribute and in which all participants share the financial resources, it should be expected that many of the church organizations will be contributors of revenue as well as recipients of financial support. This is particularly true of ladies' guilds, men's clubs, and youth groups. Any group that includes in its program some type of revenue-producing activity should consider turning over a portion of that revenue to the central church treasury to be applied against that organization's annual pledge. The practice of church departments or organizations maintaining cash funds, which sometimes run into thousands of dollars, is not consistent with the concept of a unified budget, nor with sound business management.

PLATE OFFERINGS

Plate offerings in both the sanctuary and the church school should also be subjected to considerable study and analysis. From year to year, the exact number of Sundays in the calendar, in any particular month, and the relationship of these Sunday dates to the public school year and to holidays, are subject to change. Based on experience, average amounts received at individual services at different times of the year should be determined. A figure relating these averages to the actual number of similar Sundays in the budget period should be developed and entered on the budget worksheet. It is particularly important in this connection to estimate amounts anticipated to be given on special holidays or special events in the life of the church. As these figures are entered on the budget income worksheet, any prior commitment as to specific use of the funds should also be noted.

CONTRIBUTIONS OR GIFTS

Under the heading of contributions or gifts, a distinction should be made between unrestricted gifts and restricted gifts. The unrestricted gift is that with "no strings." It is available for the use of the church wherever the need is greatest. The restricted gift, on the other hand, is one given with some particular objective in mind.

Examples of restricted contributions would include a gift restricted to the purchase of planting and landscaping services, to providing floral arrangements for the sanctuary, to obtaining kitchen equipment, or to financing a particular missionary effort. Throughout the budgetary and accounting structure, there must exist a method of maintaining the identity of restricted gifts both as to their source and the purpose for which they were given.

The inclusion of contributions or gifts in the church budget involves an element of uncertainty. It is difficult to plan for the receipt of gifts. An effort should be made, however, to recognize in the budget the possibility that such gifts might materialize.

USE OF CHURCH FACILITIES

Contributions to the church treasury often occur as an expression of appreciation in return for the use of church facilities. Examples would include the use of a neighborhood hall for community activities not directly associated with the church, or the use of church school classrooms by a day school. Such amounts should be considered as contributions made by the using activities as an indication of their honest desire to support the church.

Inclusion of such contributions in the budget should be on the basis of the pattern of previous years. The extent to which such contributions play a part in church finances is a matter of local church policy. Certainly the opening to the public of church facilities cannot be primarily conceived as a revenue-making move. To so do could involve the church in controversy as to its tax-exempt status. The offering of the facilities should be in response to the needs of the neighborhood, with any forthcoming contributions a purely secondary consideration.

ENDOWMENTS AND INVESTMENTS

Many churches are fortunate enough to have endowments and to have them combined into one or more endowment funds. Endowments also may be restricted or unrestricted, depending on the wishes of the donor. Where restrictions exist, separate endowment funds should be maintained to indicate the responsibility of the church for carrying out the terms of the endowment. Budgeting and accounting procedure must be such that the return from endowments is spent only for the stated purposes.

All endowments should be placed under the management of a trusteeship that can be expected to return a reasonable income from the investment of the endowment funds. The trustee should be bonded in an amount sufficient to cover the maximum size of the endowment during the bonding period. He should be encouraged to exercise his judgment and freedom in the investment of the funds. He should also be asked to provide the programs-and-budget committee with a forecast of income to be included in their deliberations.

SPECIAL EVENTS

The fellowship program of many churches includes activities such as suppers, bazaars, and similar affairs. Depending on the policy of the church, these functions may also be a source of revenue. Under the truly unified budget, this income passes through the established procedures of church programming, budgeting, and accounting. In some instances, this income may be covered by organizational pledges as previously described. If the concept of organizational pledging is followed, the organization is committed to raise the amount pledged. If the concept is followed of separately showing income from special activities, there is not quite the same element of commitment. Instead, there is an understanding that the amount netted on the event is available to the church treasury.

Several examples of worksheets developed for the study of church financial resources appear in Chapter 5.

STUDY OF THE OPERATING PERIOD

Careful study of past operating periods is as important in analyzing income as it is in analyzing needs. In fact, many of the entries on the income worksheet will be forecasts or projections of previous figures. As part of this process, a variance study should be made of amounts previously budgeted as income, and amounts that were actually raised. The variance, whether it be favorable or unfavorable, should be carefully analyzed.

An example of an extensive analysis of the income of a church is shown at Exhibit 10, on page 90. This exhibit should be compared to Exhibit 6, on page 68 Both are from

HOPE LUTHERAN CHURCH
ST. LOUIS, MISSOURI

EIGHT YEAR COMPARISON OF INCOME
ANALYZED IN TERMS OF PERCENTAGE OF TOTAL INCOME AND AMOUNT PER COMMUNICANT
DECEMBER 31, 1961

FISCAL YEAR	COMMUNICANT MEMBERS	(1) WEEKLY ENVELOPES	(2) LOOSE OFFERINGS	(3) SPECIAL CURRENT OFFERINGS	(4) MISSION SUNDAY	(5) ADVENT AND CHRISTMAS	(6) SPECIAL SYNODICAL OFFERINGS	(7) LUTHERAN HIGH SCHOOL BUILDING FUND	(8) DESIGNATED MISSION OFFERINGS
				AMOUNT					
1954		$ 55 690	$ 3 581	$ 8 670	$ 2 908	$ 2 214	$ 550	$ 374	$ 120
1955		58 219	4 207	7 878	2 513	2 713	4 593	5 655	1 558
1956		63 017	4 491	10 402	2 721	2 936	-0-	16 598	1 675
1957		69 674	4 863	8 760	5 122	3 026	-0-	15 332	1 837
1958		105 429	4 574	8 799	4 321	3 773	-0-	14 508	723
1959		111 754	4 135	9 683	3 737	4 248	-0-	6 259	2 590
1960		119 473	4 118	9 888	3 808	3 673	-0-	-0-	485
1961		124 917	3 593	12 010	4 389	3 675	-0-	-0-	1 293
TOTALS		$ 708 173	$ 33 562	$ 76 090	$ 29 519	$ 26 258	$ 5 143	$ 58 726	$ 10 281
				PERCENTAGE					
1954		46.1%	2.9%	7.2%	2.4%	1.8%	.5%	.3%	.1%
1955		43.5	3.1	5.9	1.9	2.0	3.4	4.2%	1.2
1956		42.8	3.0	7.1	1.8	2.0	-0-	11.3	1.1
1957		50.1	3.5	6.3	3.7	2.2	-0-	11.0	1.3
1958		71.9	3.1	6.0	2.9	2.6	-0-	9.9	.5
1959		77.0	2.9	6.7	2.6	2.9	-0-	4.3	1.7
1960		80.5	2.8	6.7	2.5	2.5	-0-	-0-	.3
1961		78.8	2.3	7.5	2.8	2.3	-0-	-0-	.8
AVERAGE		62.1%	2.9%	6.7%	2.6%	2.3%	.5%	5.1%	.9%
				AMOUNT PER COMMUNICANT					
1954	(1,404)	$ 39 65	$ 2 55	$ 6 15	$ 1 10	$ 1 60	$ 40	$ 25	$ 35
1955	(1,431)	40 75	2 95	5 50	1 75	1 90	3 20	3 95	1 05
1956	(1,501)	42 00	3 00	6 95	1 80	1 95	-0-	11 05	1 10
1957	(1,424)	48 90	3 45	6 15	3 60	2 15	-0-	10 75	1 30
1958	(1,503)	70 15	3 05	5 85	2 85	2 50	-0-	9 65	50
1959	(1,470)	76 00	2 80	6 60	2 55	2 90	-0-	4 25	1 75
1960	(1,481)	80 65	2 80	6 70	2 60	2 45	-0-	-0-	30
1961	(1,491)	83 80	2 40	8 05	2 95	2 45	-0-	-0-	85
AVERAGE	(1,463)	$ 60 50	$ 2 90	$ 6 50	$ 2 50	$ 2 25	$ 45	$ 5 00	$ 90

Exhibit 10. Example of a Detailed Analysis of Church Income
(Furnished by Hope Lutheran Church, St. Louis, Missouri.)

FISCAL YEAR	(9) DEVELOPMENT AND BUILDING FUND	(10) TOTAL OFFERINGS	(11) DAY SCHOOL TUITION AND UTILITIES	(12) RENTAL AND OTHER INCOME	(13) TOTAL INCOME	(14) INCREASE OR (DECREASE) PRIOR YEAR	(15) INCREASE OR (DECREASE) SINCE 1954
			AMOUNT				
1954	$ 43 565	$ 117 672	$ 1 800	$ 1 338	$ 120 810	$ -0-	$ -0-
1955	42 015	129 351	2 081	2 433	133 865	13 055	13 055
1956	41 294	143 134.	1 840	2 361	147 335	13 470	26 525
1957	25 861	134 475	1 325	3 209	139 009	(8 326)	18 199
1958	-0-	142 127	1 590	2 929	146 646	7 637	25 836
1959	-0-	142 406	1 282	1 396	145 084	(1 562)	24 274
1960	-0-	141 445	3 709	3 338	148 492	3 408	27 682
1961	-0-	149 877	4 397	4 258	158 532	10 040	37 722
TOTALS	$ 152 735	$1 100 487	$ 18 024	$ 21 262	$1 139 773		
			PERCENTAGE				
1954	36.1%	97.4%	1.5%	1.1%	100%	-0-	-0-
1955	31.4	96.6	1.6	1.8	100	10.8	10.8
1956	28.0	97.1	1.3	1.6	100	10.1	22.0
1957	18.6	96.7	1.0	2.3	100	(5.7)	11.5
1958	-0-	96.9	1.0	2.1	100	5.5	21.4
1959	-0-	98.1	.9	1.0	100	(1.1)	20.1
1960	-0-	95.3	2.5	2.2	100	2.3	22.9
1961	-0-	94.5	2.8	2.7	100	6.8	31.
AVERAGE	13.4%	96.5%	1.6%	1.9%	100%		
		AMOUNT PER COMMUNICANT					
1954	$ 31 00	$ 83 80	$ 1 30	$ 95	$ 86 05	$ -0-	$ -0-
1955	29 35	90 40	1 45	1 70	93 55	7 50	7 50
1956	27 50	95 35	1 25	1 55	98 15	4 60	12 10
1957	18 15	94 45	90	2 25	97 60	(55)	11 55
1958	-0-	94 55	1 05	1 95	97 55	(05)	11 50
1959	-0-	96 85	90	95	98 70	1 15	12 65
1960	-0-	95 50	2 50	2 25	100 25	1 55	14 20
1961	-0-	100 50	2 95	2 85	106 30	6 05	20 25
AVERAGE	$ 13 05	$ 94 05	$ 1 55	$ 1 80	$ 97 40		

Exhibit 10.   Continued

the annual audit report of Hope Lutheran Church, St. Louis, Missouri.

Two additional important points should be kept in mind in our study of the financial resources of the church. The first is that our work should be resourceful and imaginative. We should avoid showing, year after year, the same sources and the same amounts. Old sources of church income should be re-examined and new sources explored. The result should be a challenging and inspiring appraisal of resources that can be mobilized by churches having the energy and the inspiration to do so. Although the resource estimate should be imaginative, it must also be realistic.

The second additional point of importance is that of keeping supporters of the church informed as to the various resources of the church and the amounts realized from each. Our slogan might be, "The best informed giver is the most generous giver." Most of us are more inclined to commit ourselves to the support of a program when we have a clear picture of the support expected and the relative role our own contribution plays.

Many churches seem reluctant to publish the income portion of their budget. There should be no such reluctance. If the budget truly reflects the policy of the church in regard to sources from which it will accept revenue, those sources should be identified. If the leadership has doubts as to the propriety of some contribution, those doubts should be honestly resolved. The problem should not be avoided through omission of the item from the budget.

In Chapter 5, we shall consider the details of budget worksheet preparation. What are the essential components of a properly drafted budget document? What format is most meaningful to church officers and staff? To the membership? What time schedule should be established for orderly accomplishment of the many successive and dependent steps in church budget development?

PREPARING AND
PROCESSING BUDGET
WORKING PAPERS

WE HAVE IDENTIFIED many elements that must be considered in preparing the church budget. We have discussed an approach and philosophy useful in resolving the problems encountered. In this and the two following chapters, we will be concerned with the detailed preparation and processing of the several documents that make up a complete budget. The approach to details will not be the same in any two churches. There is no reason why it should be. We shall deal here with basic approaches that can be adopted, with local variations, in all churches.

In Chapter 1, four documents were briefly defined: the operating budget, the capital budget, the cash-flow budget, and the appeal budget. The first three are primarily working papers used by the officers, committees, and staff. The last, the appeal budget, is a version of the budget specially prepared for the general membership and the public. A well-prepared appeal budget is essential to successful fund-raising procedure.

The concept of the appeal budget is based on the belief that the average church member is not greatly interested in the myriad of details of church expense. He is interested, instead, in the major categories of expense as they relate to the significant programs and functions of the church. The preparation of the appeal budget is discussed in Chapter 6.

In the present chapter, we will cover the preparation of the operating and capital budgets. A second concern will be with the programming and budgeting calendar, the sequence and timing of actions to be accomplished. We will also consider the continuing nature of budgeting: that is, the idea that each annual budget is really only a link in a chain of budgets, each of which is based upon a predecessor and each leading in turn to a successor.

THE CALL FOR PROGRAMS
AND BUDGET ESTIMATES

The annual cycle of budget development should be initiated by a written request or "call" addressed to the heads of all church activities having financial support requirements or representing sources of income. This call should explain the necessity for early and thorough consideration of the needs of programs requesting financial support. It should also provide guidance and information as to the format and date upon which the church programs-and-budget committee requires the completed information.

A considerable advantage lies in the technique of distributing the call for estimates at a meeting conducted by the chairman of the programs-and-budget committee. Any question that might arise can be quickly addressed, or taken under consideration for future resolution. For churches in which the call for programs and budget estimates has become well established and understood, the mailing of the letter to responsible individuals is probably enough.

Attached to the written call should be the format on which submission of programs and budget estimates is desired. This form should provide for the identification of the requesting activity, an indication of the program period covered, and space for fairly detailed description of the needs of that activity. To facilitate compilation of all the requests, the form should differentiate between recurring or routine needs, and special programs involving discretionary items of expense.

Although some churches ask the submitting activity to indicate dollar amounts used in former years, this, of course, is not really essential, if such information is readily available in the records of the board of finance. Perhaps our attitude should be that each activity should be kept fully aware of its own expense, and therefore inclusion of this item on the format serves a useful educational purpose. The form should allow for adequate expression of the position of the individual activity on any new or unusual items. In all cases, the format should terminate with a clear statement that the request submitted is a carefully considered and responsible statement of programs and needs, and the signature of the head of the program or activity. An example of a program and budget request form was shown as Exhibit 3, on page 54.

THE EXPENDITURE WORKSHEET

The most detailed of the budgetary documents, and the one which will be revised and reworked the most, is the expenditure worksheet. This is the portion of the budget in which are assembled all of the needs reported in response to the call for programs and estimates, and received from other sources. The basic approach to development of this document is twofold. First, it should be compatible with the church accounting structure, so that clerical work and comparisons with operating periods will be facilitated. Secondly, it must lend itself to consolidation and rearrangement into the appeal budget, to be described in Chapter 6.

The expenditure worksheet should be set up in a business-like manner, with a masthead giving the name of the church, and the date and name of the preparing group, usually the programs-and-budget committee. The date is important because we must visualize several variations of this document, dated some weeks apart, reflecting changes in programs and estimates during the formulative period. The columns provided on the worksheet should allow for a description of each entry or item, and, if appropriate, reference to an accounting code. The columns for dollar entries must show, as a minimum, the last completed period (year), the current operating period, and the budget period. Desirable also is provision for variance columns in which may be shown increases or decreases between years.

Some churches might wish to use the technique of flexible budgeting, providing columns for two or more levels of activity in the budget period. For instance, a church might wish to project a budget at the $50,000 level and at the $60,000 level if there were some reason to think that there might be this much variation in income. Another technique is that of projecting the budget at two or more membership levels—for example, at the 210-family level, the 225-family level, and the 240-family level.

Having established the column headings, we turn our attention to the line sequence in which the various items are entered. Here also, we have many alternatives. The first would be simply to use the accounting structure, in which the various items are listed in account code sequence. A second approach, more responsive to the concept of program submission by individual activities, is that of listing organizations and activities in some logical sequence. Several possibilities are illustrated by the exhibits. Exhibit 11, on page 97, illustrates a worksheet in which the item sequence follows a standard church accounting structure. Exhibit 12, on page 106, illustrates a flexible approach in the use of columns headed "must" and "venture." The line sequence is functional.

Many denominations and local churches prefer to distinguish between "home expenses" and "benevolences." Exhibit 13, on page 108, illustrates this approach carried to the point of preparing separate but common budgets.

Account Number (As suggested in Broadman Church Finance Record System)	I. WORLD MISSIONS INCLUDING COOPERATIVE PROGRAM (200)		Weekly amount in this year's budget	Weekly amount we recommend for next year
201	**Cooperative Program**			
	The Cooperative Program is the plan of work of Southern Baptists for doing mission work in one's state, the nation, and around the world in obedience to the commands of Christ. It is the primary channel for our missionary giving.			
	Through this program, members of our church are able to participate in the missionary, educational, and benevolent work undertaken by our denomination throughout the world.			
	It is suggested that the Cooperative Program be included in our budget on the basis of a percentage of all budget receipts (undesignated), that this percentage of the total budget be at least 2 per cent more than the percentage for the current year, and that this percentage be set early in the development of the budget. (See pages one and two of this workbook.)			
	We recommend that we give during the next budget year _____ per cent of the total budget receipts (undesignated), which percentage should produce approximately this amount per week		$	$
202	**Associational Missions**			
	We recommend that we give _____ per cent of total undesignated budget receipts, which should produce approximately this amount per week		$	$
203			$	$
204			$	$
205			$	$
206			$	$
207			$	$
	TOTAL for World Missions Including Cooperative Program . . . . Carry weekly total forward to summary sheet.		X X X X	$

Exhibit 11. Program and Budget Worksheet Based Upon Church Account Numbering System

(Prepared by SBC Stewardship Services.)

Account Number		II. LOCAL MISSIONS (210)	Weekly amount in this year's budget	Weekly am~~~ we recomm~ for next y~
211		Mission pastor's salary	$	$
212		Rent and utilities	$	$
213		Literature	$	$
214		Supplies and equipment	$	$
215		Building Fund	$	$
216			$	$
217			$	$
218			$	$
219			$	$
		TOTAL for Local Missions Carry weekly total forward to summary sheet.	X X X X	$
		III. SALARIES (220)		
221		Pastor's Salary	$	$
222		Minister of Education's Salary	$	$
223		Minister of Music's Salary	$	$
224		Secretarial Salaries	$	$
225		Janitors' Salaries	$	$
226		Nursery Salaries	$	$

Exhibit 11.   Continued

Account Number		III. SALARIES (220) Continued	Weekly amount in this year's budget	Weekly amount we recommend for next year
227			$	$
228			$	$
229			$	$
		TOTAL for Salaries .... Carry weekly total forward to summary sheet.	X X X X	$
		IV. OTHER PERSONNEL EXPENSES (230)		
231		Convention Expense	$	$
232		Denominational Retirement Plan	$	$
233		Housing Allowances	$	$
234		Social Security Taxes	$	$
235			$	$
236			$	$
237			$	$
238			$	$
239			$	$
		TOTAL for Other Personnel Expense .... Carry weekly total forward to summary sheet.	X X X X	$

Exhibit 11.   Continued

Account Number		V. ORGANIZATIONAL AND EDUCATIONAL MINISTRY (240)	Weekly amount in this year's budget	Weekly amount we recommend for next year
241		Sunday School		
	241-1	Literature and Supplies	$	$
	241-2	Study Courses and Enlargement Campaigns	$	$
	241-3	Summer Assemblies and Conventions	$	$
	241-4	Promotion and Recreation	$	$
	241-5	Vacation Bible Schools	$	$
242		Training Union		
	242-1	Literature and Supplies	$	$
	242-2	Study Courses and Enlargement Campaigns	$	$
	242-3	Summer Assemblies and Conventions	$	$
	242-4	Promotion and Recreation	$	$
243		Brotherhood (Includes Royal Ambassadors)		
	243-1	Literature and Supplies	$	$
	243-2	Study Courses	$	$
	243-3	Summer Assemblies and Conventions	$	$

Exhibit 11.   Continued

Account Number		V. ORGANIZATIONAL AND EDUCATIONAL MINISTRY (240) Continued	Weekly amount in this year's budget	Weekly amount we recommend for next year
243		Brotherhood (Continued)		
	243-4	Promotion and Recreation	$	$
244		Woman's Missionary Union		
	244-1	Literature and Supplies	$	$
	244-2	Study Courses	$	$
	244-3	Summer Assemblies and Conventions	$	$
	244-4	Promotion and Recreation	$	$
245		Church Music Ministry		
	245-1	Literature and Supplies	$	$
	245-2	Study Courses	$	$
	245-3	Summer Assemblies and Conventions	$	$
	245-4	Promotion and Recreation	$	$
246		Church Library	$	$
	246-1	Books, Magazine Subscriptions, and Supplies		
	246-2	Summer Assemblies and Conventions	$	$
	246-3	Binding and Repairs	$	$

Exhibit 11.   Continued

Account Number		V. ORGANIZATIONAL AND EDUCATIONAL MINISTRY (240) Continued	Weekly amount in this year's budget	Weekly amount we recommend for next year
247		Schools of Missions or Stewardship	$	$
248		Audio-Visual Aids	$	$
249			$	$
		TOTAL for Organizational and Educational Ministry Carry weekly total forward to summary sheet.	X X X X	$
		VI. SERVICE MINISTRIES (250)		
251		Radio and TV	$	$
252		Publicity	$	$
253		Subscriptions	$	$
254		Postage, Printing, and Office Supplies	$	$
255		Annual Budget Promotion	$	$
256		Scholarships or Loan Fund for Church-Related Vocations Volunteers	$	$
257		Revival and Pulpit Supply Honoraria and Expense	$	$
258		Flowers, Special Dinners, Anniversaries, Homecomings	$	$
259		Auditing and Bonding Fees	$	$
		TOTAL for Service Ministries Carry weekly total forward to summary sheet.	X X X X	$

Exhibit 11.   Continued

count Number	VII. BUILDINGS AND EQUIPMENT (260)	Weekly amount in this year's budget	Weekly amount we recommend for next year
51	Utilities	$	$
52	Insurance	$	$
53	Taxes	$	$
54	Janitors' Supplies, Laundry, and Dry Cleaning	$	$
55	Repair and Maintenance of Existing Buildings	$	$
56	Repair and Maintenance of Existing Equipment	$	$
57	Purchase of New Equipment	$	$
58		$	$
59		$	$
	TOTAL for Buildings and Equipment Carry weekly total forward to summary sheet.	X X X X	$
	VIII. DEBT RETIREMENT (270) (Total debt at beginning of next fiscal year: $_____)		
71	Principal	$	$
72	Interest Payments	$	$
73		$	$
74		$	$
75		$	$
	TOTAL for Debt Retirement Carry weekly total forward to summary sheet.	X X X X	$

Exhibit 11. Continued

Account Number	IX. BUILDING RESERVE (280)	Weekly amount in this year's budget	Weekly amount we recommend for next year
281	To Set Aside Weekly for New Building Site	$	$
282	To Set Aside Weekly for New Auditorium	$	$
283	To Set Aside Weekly for New Educational Space	$	$
284	To Set Aside Weekly for New Pastor's Home	$	$
285	To Set Aside Weekly for New Mission Chapel(s)	$	$
286	To Set Aside for Proposed Major Remodeling and/or Equipment, such as Redecorating, Air Conditioning, etc.	$	$
287	To Set Aside Weekly for New Summer Assembly Facilities	$	$
288	To Set Aside Weekly for Architect's Fees Due This Year	$	$
289		$	$
	TOTAL for Building Reserve Carry weekly total forward to summary sheet.	X X X X	$

Exhibit 11. Continued

SUMMARY SHEET

Summary of Proposed Weekly* Budget for Coming Year, 19____

1. World Missions including Cooperative Program.. $ _____ _____ per week
2. Local Missions .... $ _____ per week
3. Salaries .... $ _____ per week
4. Other Personnel Expenses .... $ _____ per week
5. Organizational and Educational Ministry ...... $ _____ per week
6. Service Ministries .... $ _____ per week
7. Building and Equipment .... $ _____ per week
8. Debt Retirement .... $ _____ per week
9. Building Reserve .... $ _____ per week

TOTAL $ _____ PER WEEK
(Total for 52 weeks, $_____)

NOW LET'S COMPARE ...

Compare Proposed Budget with Current Budget:

1. Proposed budget for coming year, per week .... $ _____
2. Budget for the current year, per week .... $ _____
3. Increase in proposed budget per week (Subtract line 2 from line 1) .... $ _____

Compare Proportion of Budget to World Missions Through the Cooperative Program in the Two Years:

1. Percentage of total undesignated budget receipts through the Cooperative Program for the coming year .... $ _____
2. Percentage of total undesignated budget receipts through the Cooperative Program for the current year .... $ _____
3. Increase in percentage of total budget through the Cooperative Program (Subtract line 2 from line 1) .... $ _____

Compare Tithe With Proposed Budget:

1. Estimated tithe of the entire congregation per week (See FB-3, This We Are Able) .... $ _____
2. Proposed budget for coming year, per week .... $ _____
3. Difference in proposed budget and the tithe, per week (Subtract line 2 from line 1) .... $ _____

*Experience has proven it is best to use figures for the *weekly* budget goal in planning and promoting the budget, rather than the annual figure.

Exhibit 11.   Continued

PRELIMINARY PROPOSAL

Program Builder Budget Work Sheet

PART ONE—Current Program For our work within the congregation	Last Full Year's Program (Actual)	Current Year's Program (Budget)	Recommended Goals	
			Must	Venture
Ministry of the Pastor				
Salaries	$	$	$	$
Supply Pastor's Honoraria/Expenses				
Parsonage Upkeep and Modernization				
Auto Allowance (operation and replacement)				
Retirement and Health Benefits				
Book Fund				
Professional Expenses (conferences, conventions)				
Total for Pastoral Service	$	$	$	$
Ministry of Worship				
Music Salaries	$	$	$	$
Retirement and Health Benefits				
Organ and Piano Maintenance				
Choir Vestments				
Altar Supplies				
Hymn Books and Bulletins				
Total for Worship	$	$	$	$
Education and Community Outreach				
Deaconess or Parish Worker	$	$	$	$
Director of Religious Education				
Retirement and Health Benefits				
Church School				
Vacation and Weekday School				
Equipment (A-V's, tables, etc.)				
Subsidies, Conferences, etc.				
Subscriptions, "The Lutheran", etc.				
Library				
Publicity				
Fellowship Activities				
Social Ministry				
Total for Community Outreach	$	$	$	$
Parish Administration				
Secretary's Salary	$	$	$	$
Retirement and Health Benefits				
Office Equipment				
Stationery, Printing, Postage				
Telephone				
Unexpected Emergencies				
Total for Administration	$	$	$	$
Maintenance				
Sexton's Salary	$	$	$	$
Retirement and Health Benefits				
Maintenance Supplies				
Utilities and Fuel				
Property Repairs and Improvements				
Insurance (____Fidelity Bond; ____Fire; ____Public Liability; ____Workmen's Compensation; ____Burglary, Theft, Robbery; ____Boiler)				
Total for Maintenance	$	$	$	$

Exhibit 12. Program and Budget Worksheet with Flexible Goals

(Furnished by the Commission on Stewardship, The Lutheran Church in America.)

PART TWO—Benevolence Program For our work beyond the congregation	Last Full Year's Program (Actual)	Current Year's Program (Budget)	Recommended Goals	
			Must	Venture
Apportioned Benevolence, Synod & LCA	$	$	$	$
Total Apportioned Benevolence:	$	$	$	$
Unapportioned Benevolence:				
Foreign Missionary Support	$	$	$	$
Home Mission Sponsorship				
Local Council of Churches				
Inner Mission Work				
Pastor's Discretionary Fund				
Total Unapportioned Benevolence	$	$	$	$
Total Benevolence	$	$	$	$

PART THREE—Advance Program For our debt retirement and advance programs	Last Full Year's Program (Actual)	Current Year's Program (Budget)	Recommended Goals	
			Must	Venture
Capital Funds				
Payments on Debt or Mortgage	$	$	$	$
Interest Expense				
Building Fund Accumulation				
Special Projects				
Total Capital Funds	$	$	$	$

PRELIMINARY PROPOSAL SUMMARY

I Current Program
   For our work within the Congregation

Ministry of Pastor	$	$	$	$
Ministry of Worship				
Education and Community Outreach				
Parish Administration				
Property Maintenance				
Total Current Program	$	$	$	$

II Benevolence Program

For our work beyond the Congregation

Apportioned	$	$	$	$
Unapportioned				
Total Benevolences	$	$	$	$

III Advance Program

Capital Funds	$	$	$	$
Total Capital Funds	$	$	$	$
Total Proposed	$	$	$	$

Exhibit 12.   Continued

PROPOSED HOME EXPENSE BUDGET FOR 19....

Church..Place..

MINISTRY, LEADERSHIP AND SERVICE	Last Year 19....	This Year 19....	Proposed 19....
Minister	$............	$............	$............
Pulpit Supply	....	....	....
Minister's Annuity	....	....	....
Car Allowance	....	....	....
Traveling Expense (Conference, Synod)	....	....	....
Director of Religious Education	....	....	....
Organist and Choir Director	....	....	....
Church School	....	....	....
Vacation Bible School	....	....	....
Youth Work	....	....	....
Visual Aids	....	....	....
Work of Standing Committees (Stewardship and Mission- ary Education, Christian Social Action, etc.)	....	....	....
	$............	$............	$............

COST OF OPERATION			
Church Secretary	$............	$............	$............
Office Equipment	....	....	....
Telephone	....	....	....
Stationery, Printing and Supplies	....	....	....
Music	....	....	....
Library, Books and Periodicals	....	....	....
Maintenance, Organ and Piano	....	....	....
Custodian	....	....	....
Utilities, Heat, Light, Water	....	....	....
Flowers	....	....	....
Miscellaneous	....	....	....
	$............	$............	$............

MAINTENANCE AND IMPROVEMENT OF CHURCH PROPERTY			
Church Building Improvements, Repairs	$............	$............	$............
Service and Supplies	....	....	....
Indebtedness Reduction	....	....	....
Indebtedness Interest	....	....	....
Insurance	....	....	....
Parsonage Upkeep and Fuel	....	....	....
	$............	$............	$............

CAPITAL FUNDS	$............	$............	$............
RESERVED FOR CONTINGENCIES	$............	$............	$............
TOTAL............	$............	$............	$............

Exhibit 13. Worksheet for Two-Part Home Expense and Benevolence Budget

(Furnished by the Stewardship Council, United Church of Christ.)

PROPOSED 19.... BENEVOLENCE BUDGET*

A. For Our Christian World Mission

Through pledged giving in Our Christian Enlistment	1962	1963
1. National Instrumentalities (National budget, United Church of Christ)**	$....................	$....................

Executive Council, United Church of Christ
Administration, ecclesiastical and ecumenical functions
Board for World Ministries
Our agency for mission and service abroad
Board for Homeland Ministries
Our agency for church extension, evangelism, Christian
education, Christian higher education, health and welfare
Council for Social Action, Council for Lay Life and Work,
Council for Church and Ministry, Stewardship Council,
Office of Communication, Pension Boards

2. Acting Conference, United Church of Christ Ministerial placement, church extension, leadership training, liaison with national instrumentalities	....	....

Through Special Giving

3. Board for World Ministries, in One Great Hour of Sharing	....	....
4. Board for World Ministries, in Share Our Surplus	....	....
5. Conference, Board for Homeland Ministries and Board for World Ministries, in Christian Higher Education Fund	....	....

B. For Institutions Related to the United Church of Christ

6. Colleges and Seminaries	....	....
7. Health and Welfare Institutions	....	....
8. Acting Conference Non-budgeted Projects	....	....

C. For Interdenominational Ministries

9. Council of Churches (local, state, national, world)	....	....
10. United Ministries (For example, American Bible Society)	....	....
Total for All Benevolences	$....................	$....................

*For detailed discussion and recommendations see the booklet, *Preparing Your Benevolence Budget*. Order from the Stewardship Council.

**Some churches may desire a further breakdown of the national budget. In this case, divide item 1 according to the following percentages: Executive Council – 4.6%, Board for World Ministries – 37.7%, Board for Homeland Ministries – 30.4%, and Other Instrumentalities – 27.3%.

Exhibit 13.   Continued

In comparing Exhibits 11, 12, and 13, many other features of expense worksheet preparation will be noted. Outstanding among these is the difference in degree of detail and the differing approaches to comparison of past, present, and future periods. Each example should be viewed in terms of its usefulness in detailed study and decision-making. Our questions should be: Is the arrangement logical and readily understood? Is the language simple and direct? Is a place provided for remarks or explanations of unusual entries?

Because the financial situations of individual churches vary greatly, no simple format for a general worksheet can be proposed that will serve in all instances. However, the following has been found to be generally useful. It can be easily modified to meet specific needs.

GENERAL FORMAT

BUDGET WORKSHEET—EXPENDITURES

ITEM	1962 ACTUAL	1963 ESTI-MATED	1964 PLANNED
Public Worship and Pastoral Leadership	$	$	$
Minister's salary			
Minister's annuity			
Minister's allowances			
Minister's utilities			
Ass't. Minister's salary			
Ass't. Minister's annuity			
Ass't. Minister's allowances			
Ass't. Minister's utilities			
Pulpit Supply			
SUB TOTAL			

ITEM	1962 ACTUAL	1963 ESTI-MATED	1964 PLANNED
Music			
Organist, Choir Director's salary			
Sacred music purchase			
Care and replacement of robes			
Maintenance of instruments			
SUB TOTAL			
Religious Education			
Associate's salary			
Associate's allowances			
Educational materials and supplies			
Vacation church school			
Camp and conference programs			
Youth activities			
Adult classes and programs			
SUB TOTAL			
Administration			
Secretary's salary			
Clerk's salary			
Telephone			
Bonding expense			
Office supplies			
SUB TOTAL			

General Format (continued)

ITEM	1962 ACTUAL	1963 ESTI-MATED	1964 PLANNE
Property Care and Maintenance			
Custodian's wages			
Custodial supplies			
Utilities			
Insurance			
Repairs			
Improvements (list items)			
Upkeep, camp and conference grounds			
SUB TOTAL			
Promotion			
Special meetings			
Advertising and publicity			
Printing and postage			
Entertainment of conventions, conferences			
Traveling expenses of delegates— Association and conferences			
Subscriptions—periodicals			
Membership dues to organizations			
Expense of financial campaign			
SUB TOTAL			
Financial			
Debt retirement (list notes)			
Interest (list notes)			
Taxes			
Reserve for contingencies			
SUB TOTAL			

ITEM	1962 ACTUAL	1963 ESTI-MATED	1964 PLANNED
Benevolences, Apportionments, and Assessments			
Apportionments (list denominational activities)			
Missions (list activities)			
Assessments (list national, state, and city federations)			
Local charities (list activities)			
Community and social service (list activities)			
Church-related institutions (list schools, colleges, seminaries, hospitals, homes)			
Sᴜʙ Tᴏᴛᴀʟ	___	___	___
TOTAL PLANNED EXPENDITURES	$	$	$

THE INCOME WORKSHEET

Many features of the income worksheet are similar to those of the expenditure worksheet. This is true of the headings of the document, its dating, and column titles. If the programs-and-budget committee elects to prepare its expenditure worksheet on a flexible basis, or to show variance columns for purposes of comparing past, present, and future periods, the same technique should be used on the income worksheet.

Analysis of income is one of the neglected areas of church financial management. In studying materials made available by all principal religious denominations and by hundreds of local churches, very few instances were found of adequate treatment of this portion of the budget. The many considerations in income analysis were developed in some detail in Chapter 4. Using that discussion as a basis, and considering the few available examples of actual practice, the author recommends the following general format for an income worksheet. This format can easily be modified to meet specific needs.

GENERAL FORMAT

BUDGET WORKSHEET—INCOME

ITEM	1962 ACTUAL	1963 ESTI- MATED	1964 PLANNED
Pledges—Individual	$	$	$
Family units—members			
In hand			
Late			
	———	———	———
Sub-Total			
Family units—friends			
In hand			
Late			
	———	———	———
Sub-Total			
Juniors			
GROSS SUB-TOTAL			
Discount—uncollectable			
	———	———	———
NET SUB-TOTAL individual pledges			

General Format (continued)

ITEM	1962 ACTUAL	1963 ESTI-MATED	1964 PLANNED
Pledges—Organizational (list organizations)			
SUB-TOTAL organizational pledges	————	————	————
Plate offerings—Sanctuary Regular services Special Events (list events, i.e., Thanksgiving, Christmas, Easter)			
SUB-TOTAL plate offerings— Sanctuary	————	————	————
Plate offerings—Church School	$	$	$
Contributions and Gifts Unrestricted gifts (list source) Restricted gifts (list source and cause) Use of Church facilities (list activities)			
SUB-TOTAL contributions and gifts	————	————	————
Return on Invested Endowed Funds Unrestricted endowments (list)			
SUB-TOTAL unrestricted endowments	————	————	————
Restricted endowments (list fund and cause)			
SUB-TOTAL restricted endowments	————	————	————
SUB-TOTAL return on endowed funds	————	————	————

ITEM	1962 ACTUAL	1963 ESTI- MATED	1964 PLANNED
Interest Earned on deposited funds			
Special Events (list event: bazaars, suppers, etc.)			
Sub-Total receipts from special events			
Sale of Bibles, books, tracts			
TOTAL INCOME	$	$	$

THE CAPITAL BUDGET

The capital budget is the statement of investment—and intention to invest further—in the property of the church. It pertains to such items as land, leaseholds, and buildings; and to major equipment such as organs, busses, and cars.

A capital budget is prepared only on an "as necessary" basis—that is, whenever a capital expenditure is contemplated. If properly prepared, it can play a useful part in financial decision-making. It can aid in ascertaining the amount that can wisely be invested in new equipment or facilities. It can assist in establishing the most advantageous times to make capital expenditures. It can force inquiry into the types of facilities best suited to the needs of the church, and the method to be employed in providing them. Lastly, it provides a basis for control of capital expenditures.

An example of a capital budget will be found at Exhibit 14, on page 118. The exhibit illustrates a relatively simple method of displaying and studying the effect of proposed changes in capital items. In this case, the church is considering increasing its fixed assets—i.e., land, buildings, and major equipment—by $73,250. The book value of such assets would rise to $422,010. The investment in these new items would be made up of cash, including a fund gathered for purchase of a new organ, and additional sums borrowed. The latter would increase the church's total debt to $134,852 and the annual debt service expense to $16,923. The exact amount of debt service and its composition would change from year to year, a detail not given in this example. Detail sufficient for planning purposes is shown.

THE BUDGET DEVELOPMENT TIMETABLE

In our discussion of church budget development, we have reached the point at which it is appropriate to consider timing and sequence of the many related events and actions. Planning of the budget sequence must take into account all that is to be done. Enough time must be provided for the ordained and lay leadership and church staff to accomplish the actions involved, and time for the church membership to give the budget sufficient consideration and thoughtful attention.

We must avoid a "crash" approach to budget preparation. This applies from the initiation of the call for programs and estimates all the way through to final approval. Everything possible should be done to avoid the accusation—by boards, committees, or individuals—that time was not permitted to adequately develop material or to present positions and justifications. Maurice Stans, a one-time Director of the Bureau of the Budget in the Executive Office of the President of the United States, is credited with the remark that "budgeting is the science of distributing dissatisfaction uniformly." Much of the dissatisfaction that seems to be inherent in the budgeting process can be overcome if adequate time is allowed for all concerned to receive fair consideration.

An important point apparently not recognized by some churches is the necessity for a specific occasion on which the budget is approved and accepted as both a commitment and

CAPITAL BUDGET

PROPOSED CHANGES IN LAND, BUILDINGS, AND EQUIPMENT FOR FISCAL YEAR 196

		Description	Cost	Source Cash	Note
1.		LAND AND BUILDINGS			
	a.	Existing land and buildings	$ 316,197	$ 36,197	$ 280,00
	b.	Additional parsonage to be occupied by new assistant minister. A modern, 3 bedroom home in immediate church vicinity	22,750	2,750	20,000
	c.	New service building for storage of maintenance equipment, Boy Scout property, similar items.	3,500	3,500	
		SUB-TOTAL	$ 342,447	$ 42,447	$ 300,000
2.		EQUIPMENT			
	a.	Existing equipment	$ 32,563	$ 14,563	$ 18,00
	b.	Procure and install new organ for sanctuary	47,000	18,000*	29,000
		SUB-TOTAL	$ 79,563	$ 32,563	$ 47,000
		TOTAL	$ 422,010	$ 75,010	$ 347,000

*Estimated amount in organ replacement fund as of July 1, 1963.

Exhibit 14. Example of a Capital Budget

Note Balance			Annual Debt Service		
Existing	New	Total	Interest	Retirement	Total
85,852		$ 85,852	$ 3,160	$ 8,457	$ 11,617
	20,000	20,000	424	1,112	1,536
85,852	$ 20,000	$ 105,852	$ 3,584	$ 9,569	$ 13,153
	29,000	29,000	940	2,830	3,770
0	$ 29,000	$ 29,000	$ 940	$ 2,830	$ 3,770
85,852	$ 49,000	$ 134,852	$ 4,524	$ 12,399	$ 16,923

Exhibit 14. Continued

an authority to proceed. In many churches, the constitution or by-laws require that this be voted by the assembled congregation. Whether required or optional, the idea of a point of commitment in support of a budget is extremely important and should be a key event in any budget timetable. The fact that the budget has been approved and adopted should appear as a matter of record on the budget documents, in the form of a date and a responsible signature. In the author's examination of the many budgets gathered in connection with the preparation of this book, only one carried this important entry.

To insure budget development in a timely manner, there should be a timetable establishing a date for each successive action, and perhaps indicating responsibility for each. Following is an excellent example of such a timetable.* This timetable recognizes the overlapping nature of the budget cycle. It provides for the establishment of the successor programs and budget committee, and for the posting of the

DATE	PROCESS	WHO IS RESPON-SIBLE	FUNCTION
By June 1, 1962	Name Programs and Budget Committee (PBC)	Chief Lay Official	Planning and Authorization
June 1-15, 1962	Organization meeting of PBC for allocation of tasks and analysis of objectives	Chairman, PBC	Planning
October 1-15, 1962	Review of first quarter of current year's operations	PBC	Guidance and Control

---

* Based on a paper by Julian Feldman, Executive Director of the Washington Hebrew Congregation. The paper was presented May 10, 1962, at the Institute on Church Finance sponsored by The American University, Washington, D.C.

DATE	PROCESS	WHO IS RESPON- SIBLE	FUNCTION
By October 15, 1962	Alert operating departments (OD) and subdepartments to areas of divergence from over-all budget and cash-flow pattern	PBC and OD	Guidance and Control
By October 30, 1962	Develop plans for future programs	OD	Planning
By December 1, 1962	Formulate programs for next budget year	OD	Planning
January 2-15, 1963	Review first half year of operations for conformity to budget and cash-flow, and develop budget adjustments	PBC and OD	Control, Guidance, and Authorization
February 1-28, 1963	Call for programs and budget estimates for 1963-64	PBC Chairman	Planning
March 5-15, 1963	Formulate working expenditure budget for departments for 1963-64	OD and Chief Financial Officer	Planning
March 1-20, 1963	Formulate working income projection	Board of Finance and Treasurer	Planning and Guidance
By March 25, 1963	Review and consolidate projected OD budgets	PBC	Planning
April 1, 1963	Complete hearings on individual OD budgets for justification and explanation	PBC	Planning, Guidance, and Authorization

DATE	PROCESS	WHO IS RESPON-SIBLE	FUNCTION
By April 10, 1963	Revise OD and consolidated budgets (pare down or increase)	PBC and Board of Finance	Planning
April 15, 1963	Consider, evaluate, modify, and approve consolidated budget as submitted by PBC in light of third quarter operating experience and latest income projections	Church Council	Planning and Authorization
By May 1, 1963	Distribute appeal budget to congregation	Chairman, Board of Finance	Information
May 15, 1963	Submit budget at meeting of congregation for approval	Chief Lay Official	Authorization
By June 1, 1963	Name new programs-and-budget committee	Chief Lay Official	Planning
By June 30, 1963	Post approved budget on books of account	Financial Sec. or Clerk	Authorization

newly approved budget to the books of account at the beginning of the operating period. The dates illustrate a current operating period of July 1, 1962-June 30, 1963, and a budget period of July 1, 1963-June 30, 1964.

Two documents remain to be prepared: the appeal version of the operating budget, and the cash-flow budget. These will be taken up in the following two chapters.

Chapter 6

PREPARING THE APPEAL BUDGET

PERHAPS THE MOST interesting and challenging step in the budgetary process is the conversion of the expenditure and income worksheets into the language and format of the appeal budget. Here lies a genuine opportunity for the imaginative and resourceful programs-and-budget committee. The challenge is to reflect honestly and adequately the many items that make up the budget in a way that brings out the objectives and accomplishments visualized, rather than the financial detail.

Many churches do not go to the trouble of developing appeal versions of their budgets. It is from members of these churches that we hear complaints that the budget is dull and detailed, and therefore seldom studied, if even read. This objection is overcome in a properly prepared appeal budget, in which the detail is minimized and the language with which the programs and estimates are advanced is carefully chosen. In addition to careful choice of language, the effort should be toward conciseness and brevity. The extent to which this can be done is seen in Exhibits 15 and 16, on pages 124 and 125, in which worksheet budgets running to many pages have been reduced to appeal budgets that can be printed on a pocket-size card.

METROPOLITAN MEMORIAL

The National Methodist Church

CHURCH BUDGET

For

June 1, 1962 to May 31, 1963

Budget

JUNE 1, 1962 to May 31, 196․

MINISTERIAL EXPENSE
Minister, Assistant Minister, Bishop, District
Superintendent, Pulpit Supply .... $

MUSIC EXPENSE
Director, Organist Supply, Quartets, Organ
Care, Sheet Music, Miscellaneous ....

PROPERTY EXPENSE
Church Debt—Principal and Interest; Repairs,
Insurance, Caretakers, Maintenance Supplies,
Heat, Light, Gas, Curtailment of Debts...........

OPERATION EXPENSE
Business Manager, Secretaries, Printing, Post-
age, Advertising, Telephone, Stationery, Fellowship Fund, Auto Expenses, Social Security,
Miscellaneous ....

PARSONAGES
Minister—Heat, Water, Insurance, Mainten-
ance, Furnishings ....
Assistant Minister—Furnishings, D. C. Real
Property Tax, Maintenance, Utilities ....

CHURCH SCHOOL
Minister of Christian Education, Rent, Furnishings, Utilities, Auto Expense, Church
School, Choir Director, Secretarial Help, Stationery ....

BENEVOLENCES
Commission on World Service and Finance,
Board of Missions and Church Extension,
Board of Child Care, and Other Benevolent
Needs ....
CONTINGENT FUND ....

TOTAL BUDGET $․

ESTIMATED INCOME
To Be Received from Active Pledges......
Special Offerings and Contributions......
                                         $․

Amount Needed to Meet the
   Budget .... $

Exhibit 15.   Example of an Appeal Budget of a Larger Church

(Metropolitan Memorial, The National Methodist Church, Washington, D.C.)

FIRST PRESBYTERIAN CHURCH

Manitowoc, Wisconsin

OUR PROPOSED 1961 BUDGET

RDSHIP PLEDGE A Tithe	MINIMUM PLEDGE 2.5% of your income	
	Proposed 1961	Change from 1960
ASTORAL MINISTRY	$15,273	None
ERVICE OF WORSHIP ir directors, organists, ic supplies and bulletins	$ 2,500	None
DMINISTRATIVE EXPENSE ice Secretary, Treasurer, istant Treasurer, Social urity and office supplies	$ 6,280	- $ 350
PERATING EXPENSE todian, Utilities, Fuel, urance, Janitor's supplies, ntenance and Improvements	$15,580	+ $2,475
ENEVOLENCE AND PER CAPITA TAX ludes Synod Causes Budget s year (Carroll College, Campus istry, Presbyterian Homes Foun- ion, Camps and Conferences, consin Council of Churches)	$12,706	+ $ 940
HRISTIAN EDUCATION istian Education Committee, sbyterian Life, Confirmation, ss Banquet, Scholarship Fund, ferences and Dinners	$ 1,670	- $ 355
ASTORS' HOMES	$ 1,891	- $ 235
TOTAL MINIMUM BUDGET	$56,000	
INCREASE OVER 1960		+ $2,475

Exhibit 16. Example of an Appeal Budget of a Smaller Church

Two techniques are suggested for "translating" large dollar amounts into figures more easily comprehended by most of us. They are the "pie" and the "per-family" ideas.

In the "pie" technique, a portion of the appeal budget, or a separate statement, reads this way:

Out of every dollar:

$ .24 is for benevolences and outreach programs;

   .30 pays the minister and costs of our services of worship

   .18 pays for our church school and our youth program;

   .16 pays for maintaining and improving our church property and for utilities;

   .12 pays for administrative and office expense.

$1.00

This can be graphically portrayed very simply as a "pie" chart.

In the "per-family" or "per-capita" approach, a column or remark is added to the appeal budget in which the total amounts are divided by the number of families, or the number of individuals, furnishing financial support. The result is an easily understood and appreciated dollar amount per family. An illustration of the effective use of this technique will be found at Exhibit 17, on page 127.

It will be noted from the exhibits that some churches state their appeal in the form of objectives, whereas others state their appeal in the language of responsibility. Some are inclined to stress the programs to be accomplished from an organizational point of view, whereas others retain a functional arrangement.

Whereas the expenditure and income worksheets and the cash-flow schedule are documents that are usually prepared on accounting paper and, if reproduced, are probably mimeographed, the appeal budget is attractively presented, sometimes to the extent of professional layout and design. This

Temple Israel Center

ANNUAL REPORT AND BUDGET

	Actual Expenditures 5/1/57 to 4/30/58	Anticipated Expenditures 5/1/58 to 4/30/59
RITUAL *Salaries of the Rabbi, Cantors, Ritual Director, Choir and Organist, cost of High Holiday services and religious articles*	$ 53,265.21	$ 63,000.00
BUILDING OPERATIONS AND MAINTENANCE *Porters' salaries, cost of repairs, building supplies, heat, light, mortgage interest, insurance, new school maintenance*	33,847.66	45,300.00
ADMINISTRATION *Salaries of Executive Director, office personnel, cost of bulletin, telephone, printing, stationery, postage, office supplies, United Synagogue dues, 50th Anniversary expense, loan interest*	36,920.08	51,000.00
EDUCATION . . . . NET COST *Salaries of Educational Director, school secretary, teachers, cost of books and supplies (after deducting receipts from tuition fees)* ..	29,387.59	32,800.00
PHYSICAL EDUCATION ACTIVITIES *Salary of Physical Education Director, gym equipment and supplies*	2,285.69	2,300.00
YOUTH ACTIVITIES *Salaries of full time Youth Director, professional club leaders, miscellaneous expenses*	9,369.08	13,800.00
ADULT EDUCATION *Lecturers' salaries and sundry supplies and expenses*	2,600.00	3,000.00
AMORTIZATION OF MORTGAGES & LOANS	26,296.95	34,500.00
FURNITURE & EQUIPMENT	9,278.60	....
TOTAL COST	$203,250.86	$245,700.00

Based on a membership of 1000 families, the average cost per family in maintaining our congregation next year will be $246.

In addition to budgetary requirements we are committed to capital expenditures in excess of $100,000 in repayment of outstanding loans and major repairs and improvements.

Exhibit 17. Example of an Appeal Budget With Cost-Per-Family Feature

(Furnished by Temple Israel Center, White Plains, New York.)

Exhibit 18. Example of an Income and Expenditures Worksheet

(Rock Spring Congregational Church of Arlington, Virginia.)

ROCK SPRING CONGREGATIONAL CHURCH

INCOME AND EXPENDITURES, 1960-1963

	1960 Actual	1961 Actual	1962 Actual	1963 Proposed
INCOME				
Individual Pledges	$ 42,891	$ 46,508	$ 48,335	$ 58,000
Less Reserve				2,050
Net	42,891	46,508	48,335	55,950
Church & Church School Offerings	4,160	4,052	3,928	3,800
Use of Neighborhood House	2,600	2,902	2,563	2,750
Special Offerings & Other Gifts	2,585	2,726	3,661	2,500
TOTAL INCOME	$ 52,235	$ 56,188	$ 58,487	$ 65,000

Exhibit 18. Continued

EXPENDITURES

Benevolences & Conference Support

Our Christian World Mission	3,867	4,756	7,797	7,800
Christian Higher Education Fund	3,195	3,195		
Middle Atlantic Conference	273	295	236	250
Wash. Assn., United Church of Christ	145	323	275	335
United Church of Christ Home			425	1,640
Councils of Churches	320	320	470	770
Congregational Building Society				1,000
Miscellaneous	224			455
SUB-TOTAL	8,024	10,214	9,444	12,250

Worship & Pastoral Leadership

Minister's Salary	5,800	6,200	6,300	6,660
Minister's Annuity	660	622	706	740
Minister's Allowances	750	880	900	900
Minister's Utilities	357	613	702	700
Ass't. Minister's Salary			2,240	4,300
Ass't. Minister's Annuity			282	525
Ass't. Minister's Allowances			208	400
Ass't. Minister's Utilities			121	370
Ass't. Minister's Recruiting & Moving		449	501	
Pulpit Supply	160	175	75	
Organist & Choir Director	1,849	1,860	2,086	2,160
Board of Music	188	163	403	420
Board of Deacons	877	832	1,363	1,265
Social Action Committee		25	44	50
Rock Spring News	1,653	1,725	1,743	1,750
Reserve for Salary Adjustments				360
SUB-TOTAL	12,294	13,544	17,673	20,600

Exhibit 18. Continued

Youth Work			
Associate's Salary	4,136	4,300	3,910	4,000
Associate's Allowances	200	322	300	390
Church School Materials	2,106	1,386	931	1,225
Other Youth Activities		550	189	500
SUB-TOTAL	6,442	6,558	5,330	6,115
Church Operations				
Secretarial Services	3,253	3,425	3,319	3,165
Office Expenses	967	1,034	819	800
Telephone	728	585	763	800
Social Security Taxes	356	382	384	435
SUB-TOTAL	5,304	5,426	5,285	5,200
Church Property				
Custodial Services	3,126	3,249	3,246	3,300
Repairs & Maintenance	1,504	1,619	1,662	2,160
Utilities	3,095	3,374	3,059	3,400
Insurance	879	830	948	950
Improvements & Capital Equipment	482	225	86	445
SUB-TOTAL	9,086	9,297	9,001	10,255
Debt Service				
Interest	3,685	3,184	3,160	3,115
Debt Retirement	6,131	7,884	8,458	7,465
SUB-TOTAL	9,816	11,068	11,618	10,580
TOTAL EXPENDITURES	$ 50,966	$ 56,107	$ 58,351	$ 65,000

is necessary because this document—the appeal budget—becomes a basis for the every-member canvass and other fund-raising procedures. The appeal budget should make a favorable and lasting impression on those into whose hands it is placed.

Let us compare a detailed worksheet and an appeal budget of the same church, for the same fiscal period. The worksheet version of the 1963 budget for the author's church is shown as Exhibit 18, on page 128. The appeal version of the same budget is shown as Exhibit 19, on page 131. The worksheet version contains 46 item or object titles, and 184 dollar entries. The appeal budget contains 13 item or object titles and 27 dollar entries.

The use of an appeal budget similar to those shown as Exhibits 15, 16, 17, and 19 is highly recommended.

In Chapter 7, we shall turn again to a "working document," the cash-flow schedule (or financial plan). We shall be concerned with the questions: "How can we plan for seasonal fluctuations in income and expenditures?" and "How can we forecast financial condition for use in programming and budgeting?"

Exhibit 19. Example of an Appeal Budget (shown on following pages 132, 133)

Exhibit 19. Example of an Appeal Budget

(Rock Spring Congregational Church of Arlington, Virginia. This exhibit should be contrasted to Exhibit 18.)

ROCK SPRING CONGREGATIONAL CHURCH

<u>OUR OBJECTIVES AND OBLIGATIONS FOR THE YEAR 1963</u>

	Proposed for 1963	Change from 1962

OUR WORLD-WIDE CONCERNS: Our Objective - to increase support of our denominational ministries to the nation and the world, of interdenominational associations, and of our local church efforts, including the United Church Home.
Our Obligation: For these benevolent purposes

$ 11,250. + $1,850.

OUR PASTORAL MINISTRY: Our Objective: To provide two full time ordained ministers to lead us in worship, to counsel with us individually and to witness our Christian concerns in the community at large.
Our Obligation: For salaries, annuities, car expenses and housing

14,595. + 2,590.

OUR SERVICE OF WORSHIP AND DEACON'S ACTIVITIES: Our Objective: to provide professional direction of our choirs, to maintain the organ and pianos, to make devotional aids available to the congregation, including a subscription to the United Church Herald for each family, and to make our activities known to the congregation and the community through the Rock Spring News and newspapers advertising.
Our Obligation: For the salary of the organist-choir director and for the expenses of the activities supervised by the Board of Deacons, the Board of Music, and the Social Action Committee

5,645. - 150.

Exhibit 13. Continued

OUR CHRISTIAN EDUCATION: Our Objective: To retail a full time Director of Christian Education to provide leadership for the Church School, the Pilgrim Fellowship Groups, and the Vacation Church School.
Our Obligation: For the salary and expenses of the Director, for curriculum materials, and other Christian Education activities.   6,115. + 455.

OUR ADMINISTRATIVE SUPPORT: Our Objective: to provide the professional staff with secretarial assistance and office support.
Our obligation: For the salary of the secretary, for office supplies, telephone service and Social Security taxes.   5,200. - 145.

OUR CHURCH PROPERTY: Our Objective: To meet our financial obligations pertaining to the Church buildings and grounds, to provide full-time custodial services, maintenance, repairs, and utilities.
Our Obligation: For payment of interest and principal, custodian's salary, maintenance supplies, utilities, insurance, alterations and improvements.   20,835. + 1,455.

RESERVED FOR COUNCIL ALLOCATION: Our Obligation: To hold funds available for possible salary adjustments for the members of the staff who joined us in 1962 and to begin repayment of grants from the Congregational Building Society.   1,360. + 1,360.

TOTAL BUDGET PROPOSAL $65,000. + $7,415.

EXPECTED SOURCES OF FINANCIAL SUPPORT FOR THE YEAR 1962
Church and Church School Offerings. $ 3,800.
Special Offerings--One Great Hour of Sharing and Share Our Surplus   1,600.
Contributions for Use of Neighborhood House   2,750.
Gifts from friends of the church.   650.
                                                                         $ 8,800.

Pledges Required $58,000.
Less Reserve for uncollected pledges   1,800.
                                                         56,200.

TOTAL INCOME TO MEET BUDGET $65,000.
INCREASE OVER 1962 INCOME   + 7,415.
INCREASE OVER 1962 PLEDGES   + 8,050.

(A more detailed financial statement of proposed expenditures is available for those requesting it.)

Chapter 7

PLANNING CASH FLOW

THUS FAR WE have treated each item of expenditure and income as an annual total. Now we consider how these annual figures can be broken down into amounts for more manageable periods, such as quarters or months, for more detailed financial planning.

Churches, with their fluctuating monthly incomes, are highly vulnerable to difficulties arising from occasional periods of low financial capability. What church has not experienced periods during vacation months when the bank balance approached zero and receipts from pledges and plate offerings all too clearly reflected the absence of a large part of the congregation? The cash-flow schedule is a managerial device by which problems of periods of low financial capability are identified and solved. The underlying idea involves spreading expenditures over the fiscal year in such a way as to avoid financial emergencies and problems. This may be done in terms of quarters, or of months, or even of weeks. The discussion which follows is in terms of months.

SCHEDULING FLOW OF CASH

The schedule to be developed must be capable of fulfilling the following purposes:

First, it must indicate as closely as possible the cash receipts and disbursements that are expected to result from the programs and budgets upon which they are based, and the cash balances that will be available during each month throughout the budget period.

Second, it must clearly indicate the times at which additional funds will be needed, their amounts, and the duration of the need.

Third, it must provide information by means of which the financial condition of the church at the end of the operating period may be estimated—this estimate becoming the foundation for the programming and budgeting of the subsequent year.

The cash-flow schedule assists in tying various elements of the programs to the specific periods during the year in which they are to be accomplished, or rather, at which time they can best be accomplished from a financial point of view. As this is also a working paper, not normally distributed to the congregation as a whole, it should be prepared in a format using the language and sequence of itemization of the church accounting structure and the working version of the over-all operating budget. This format is illustrated in Exhibit 20, on page 138.

An illustration of the use made of the cash-flow schedule is seen in Exhibits 20 and 21, which show a "before and after" effect. Both are based on itemization and dollar amounts taken from Exhibit 18. Thus, Exhibits 18, 19, and 21 may be studied as a representative set of end products of one church's procedure.

Exhibit 20 is a recording of anticipated income and expense items taken from the basic church budget. These items are divided into monthly amounts on the basis of past experience or shown in periods in which customarily paid, but without considering total impact in any one period. Thus, we see in Exhibit 20 an expense item of $950 for a property insurance premium appearing in July, and an item of $720 for repairs to the church building appearing in

September. Also, on the receipts portion of Exhibit 20, we see semiannual $1,000 amounts, each of which include $900 from a local cooperative school for the use of a parish house. These amounts normally are received in October and April.

The impact of the total of these various combinations of receipts and expenses is shown on the month and cumulative balance lines at the bottom of the form. It can easily be seen that financial capability during August through November will not cover expenditures as originally entered.

In Exhibit 21, on page 142, the individual items of income and expenditures shown in Exhibit 20 have been reconsidered. Now, attention is paid to the timing of receipts and expenses. By arrangement with the various interested parties, some items have been moved into periods more appropriate for receipt or payment. This involved a new schedule of quarterly remission for world missions, a different due date for an insurance premium, and negotiation with the contractor regarding payment of his bill for repairs. Similar arrangements have been made with the cooperative school, and now the church receives the school's two major payments in September and March.

Our example here has been simplified to indicate the rearrangement of only a few items of the budget. However, the result of such actions is quite clear and can best be appreciated by observing the difference between the monthly and cumulative totals across the bottoms of the two exhibits.

An additional point to be seen in Exhibit 21 is that while the cash-flow schedule is for a single fiscal year, it is part of an annual sequence. The beginning and ending figures for the cumulative position shown on the bottom line are the same figures that appear at the end and beginning of the cash-flow schedules for the preceding and following years.

When preparing the cash-flow schedule, as in developing the basic operating budget itself, we take cognizance of items that are discretionary and those which are nondiscre-

Item	Total	Jan	Feb	Mar	Apr
INCOME					
Individual Pledges	$ 58,000				
Less Reserve	2,050				
Net	$ 55,950	$ 5,100	$ 5,100	$ 6,450	$ 5,200
Church & Church School Offerings	3,800	350	350	400	350
Use of Neighborhood House	2,750	100	100	150	1,000
Special Offerings & Other Gifts	2,500	600	200	200	350
TOTAL INCOME	65,000	6,150	5,750	7,200	6,900
EXPENDITURES					
Benevolences & Conference Support					
Our Christian World Mission	7,800	1,950			1,950
Middle Atlantic Conference	250			250	
Wash. Assn., United Church of Christ	335				335
United Church of Christ Home	1,640				
Council of Churches	770		385		
Congregational Building Society	1,000	500			
Miscellaneous	455		200	25	
SUB-TOTAL	12,250	2,450	585	275	2,285
Worship & Pastoral Leadership					
Minister's Salary	6,660	555	555	555	555
Minister's Annuity	740			740	
Minister's Allowances	900	75	75	75	75
Minister's Utilities	700	70	70	70	70
Ass't. Minister's Salary	4,300	350	350	350	350
Ass't. Minister's Annuity	525				
Ass't. Minister's Allowances	400	33	33	33	33
Ass't. Minister's Utilities	370	40	40	40	40
Organist & Choir Director	2,160	216	216	216	216
Board of Music	420		210		

Exhibit 20.   Cash-Flow Schedule Showing Original Entries

May	June	July	Aug	Sept	Oct	Nov	Dec
$ 5,200	$ 3,500	$ 2,400	$ 2,200	$ 4,100	$ 4,800	$ 5,100	$ 6,800
350	200	200	200	250	300	350	500
100	100				1,000	100	100
					150	400	600
5,650	3,800	2,600	2,400	4,350	6,250	5,950	8,000
		1,950		1,950			
820						820	
				385			
		500					
	30				100		100
820	30	2,450	0	385	2,050	820	100
555	555	555	555	555	555	555	555
75	75	75	75	75	75	75	75
70	35	35	35	35	70	70	70
350	350	350	350	350	350	350	450
				525			
33	33	33	33	33	33	33	37
40	15	10	10	15	40	40	40
216	216			216	216	216	216
				210			

Exhibit 20. Continued

Board of Deacons	1,265	100	100	100	15(
Social Action Committee	50			25	
Bulletin	1,750	160	160	160	16(
Reserve for Salary Adjustments	360				
SUB-TOTAL	20,600	1,599	1,809	2,364	1,64<u> </u>
Youth Work					
Associate's Salary	4,000	333	333	333	33]
Associate's Allowances	390	32	32	32	3:
Church School Materials	1,225		500		
Other Youth Activities	500	50	50	50	5(
SUB-TOTAL	6,115	415	915	415	41]
Office Operations					
Secretarial Services	3,165	260	260	260	26(
Office Expenses	800	70	70	70	7(
Telephone	800	67	67	67	6]
Social Security Taxes	435	36	36	36	3(
SUB-TOTAL	5,200	433	433	433	43]
Property					
Custodial Services	3,300	275	275	275	27]
Repairs & Maintenance	2,160	200	100	100	34(
Utilities	3,400	400	400	400	40(
Insurance	950				
Improvements & Capital Equipment	445		250		
SUB-TOTAL	10,255	875	1,025	775	1,0]
Debt Service					
Interest	3,115	259	259	259	25]
Debt Retirement	7,465	622	622	622	62:
SUB-TOTAL	10,580	881	881	881	88]
TOTAL EXPENDITURES	65,000	6,653	5,648	5,143	6,67]
CASH BALANCE - MONTH		- 503	+ 102	+2,057	+ 22:
CASH BALANCE - CUMULATIVE	$ 1,020*	$ 517	$ 619	$ 2,676	$ 2,89]

*Prior year's closing balance.

Exhibit 20. Continued

100	100	50	50	100	100	150	165
					25		
160	160	75	75	160	160	160	160
				90	90	90	90
1,599	1,539	1,183	1,183	2,364	1,714	1,739	1,858
333	333	333	333	333	333	333	337
32	32	32	32	32	32	32	38
225			500				
50	50			50	50	50	50
640	415	365	865	415	415	415	425
260	260	260	260	260	260	260	305
70	70	50	50	70	70	70	70
67	67	65	65	67	67	67	67
36	36	36	36	36	36	36	39
433	433	411	411	433	433	433	481
275	275	275	275	275	275	275	275
100	100	100	100	720	100	100	100
400	50	50	50	50	400	400	400
		950					
195							
970	425	1,375	425	1,045	775	775	775
259	259	259	259	259	259	259	266
622	622	622	622	622	622	622	623
881	881	881	881	881	881	881	889
5,343	3,723	6,665	3,765	5,523	6,268	5,063	4,528
+ 307	+ 77	-4,065	-1,365	-1,173	- 18	+ 887	+3,472
$ 3,205	$ 3,282	$- 783	$-2,148	$-3,321	$-3,339	$-2,452	$ 1,020

Exhibit 20. Continued

Item	Total	Jan	Feb	Mar	A
INCOME					
Individual Pledges	$ 58,000				
Less Reserve	2,050				
Net	$ 55,950	$ 5,100	$ 5,100	$ 6,450	$ 5,
Church & Church School Offerings	3,800	350	350	400	
Use of Neighborhood House	2,750	100	100	1,050	
Special Offerings & Other Gifts	2,500	600	200	200	
TOTAL INCOME	·65,000	6,150	5,750	8,100	6,
EXPENDITURES					
Benevolences & Conference Support					
Our Christian World Mission	7,800			1,950	
Middle Atlantic Conference	250			250	
Wash. Assn., United Church of Christ	335				
United Church of Christ Home	1,640				
Council of Churches	770		385		
Congregational Building Society	1,000	500			
Miscellaneous	455		200	25	
SUB-TOTAL	12,250	500	585	2,225	
Worship & Pastoral Leadership					
Minister's Salary	6,660	555	555	555	
Minister's Annuity	740			740	
Minister's Allowances	900	75	75	75	
Minister's Utilities	700	70	70	70	
Ass't. Minister's Salary	4,300	350	350	350	
Ass't. Minister's Annuity	525				
Ass't. Minister's Allowances	400	33	33	33	
Ass't. Minister's Utilities	370	40	40	40	
Organist & Choir Director	2,160	216	216	216	
Board of Music	420		210		

Exhibit 21. Completed Cash-Flow Schedule

May	June	July	Aug	Sept	Oct	Nov	Dec
$ 5,200	$ 3,500	$ 2,400	$ 2,200	$ 4,100	$ 4,800	$ 5,100	$ 6,800
350	200	200	200	250	300	350	500
100	100			900	100	100	100
					150	400	600
5,650	3,800	2,600	2,400	5,250	5,350	5,950	8,000
	1,950			1,950			1,950
820						820	
					385		
		500					
					100		100
820	1,980	500	0	1,950	485	820	2,050
555	555	555	555	555	555	555	555
75	75	75	75	75	75	75	75
70	35	35	35	35	70	70	70
350	350	350	350	350	350	350	450
					525		
33	33	33	33	33	33	33	37
40	15	10	10	15	40	40	40
216	216			216	216	216	216
				210			

Exhibit 21.   Continued

Board of Deacons	1,265	100	100	100	1
Social Action Committee	50			25	
Bulletin	1,750	160	160	160	1
Reserve for Salary Adjustments	360				
SUB-TOTAL	20,600	1,599	1,809	2,364	1,6
Youth Work					
Associate's Salary	4,000	333	333	333	3
Associate's Allowances	390	32	32	32	
Church School Materials	1,225		500		
Other Youth Activities	500	50	50	50	
SUB-TOTAL	6,115	415	915	415	
Office Operations					
Secretarial Services	3,165	260	260	260	
Office Expenses	800	70	70	70	
Telephone	800	67	67	67	
Social Security Taxes	435	36	36	36	
SUB-TOTAL	5,200	433	433	433	
Property					
Custodial Services	3,300	275	275	275	
Repairs & Maintenance	2,160	200	100	100	
Utilities	3,400	400	400	400	
Insurance	950				
Improvements & Capital Equipment	445		250		
SUB-TOTAL	10,255	875	1,025	775	1
Debt Service					
Interest	3,115	259	259	259	
Debt Retirement	7,465	622	622	622	
SUB-TOTAL	10,580	881	881	881	
TOTAL EXPENDITURES	65,000	4,703	5,648	7,093	4
CASH BALANCE - MONTH		+1,447	+ 102	+1,007	+1
CASH BALANCE - CUMULATIVE	$ 1,020*	$ 2,467	$ 2,569	$ 3,576	$ 4

*Prior year's closing balance.

Exhibit 21. Continued

100	100	50	50	100	100	150	165
					25		
160	160	75	75	160	160	160	160
				90	90	90	90
1,599	1,539	1,183	1,183	1,839	2,239	1,739	1,858
333	333	333	333	333	333	333	337
32	32	32	32	32	32	32	38
225			250	250			
50	50			50	50	50	50
640	415	365	615	665	415	415	425
260	260	260	260	260	260	260	305
70	70	50	50	70	70	70	70
67	67	65	65	67	67	67	67
36	36	36	36	36	36	36	39
433	433	411	411	433	433	433	481
275	275	275	275	275	275	275	275
100	100	100	100	100	100	100	720
400	50	50	50	50	400	400	400
						950	
195							
970	425	425	425	425	775	1,725	1,395
259	259	259	259	259	259	259	266
622	622	622	622	622	622	622	623
881	881	881	881	881	881	881	889
5,343	5,673	3,765	3,515	6,193	5,228	6,013	7,098
+ 307	-1,873	-1,165	-1,115	- 943	+ 122	- 63	+ 902
$ 5,155	$ 3,282	$ 2,117	$ 1,002	$ 59	$ 181	$ 118	$ 1,020

Exhibit 21. Continued

tionary. The nondiscretionary items should be entered first in the cash-flow schedule because, for the most part, they are quite solidly fixed both as to amount and timing. After the nondiscretionary items are entered, the discretionary items are posted. Resourcefulness is used in arranging them over the months so as to give the best results.

FORECASTING THE FINANCIAL CONDITION OF THE CHURCH

An important part of all budgetary activity is the establishment, as early as possible, of the estimated position for the end of the operating period, which also is the position for the beginning of the subsequent program period. With the operating budget and the cash-flow budget in hand, and with information available from the records of the financial secretary and the treasurer, our next step is to prepare what is called a *pro forma* treasurer's report. By this is meant a treasurer's report as we think it will appear at the end of the budget period.

Budgetary activity does not await the end of the operating period. In fact, much of it precedes by many months the end of the period. Therefore, our work is done by using estimated, or *pro forma,* positions. As seen in Exhibit 22, page 147, the *pro forma* treasurer's report resembles the actual treasurer's report that might be expected at the end of any operating period. There are two exceptions. First, it is clearly labeled *pro forma,* and, second, the dollar amounts are estimates.

This completes the major steps in preparing the church budget. We have discussed a "family" of budgetary documents. The basic document we studied was the operating budget, with its two sections, expenditures and income. The operating budget was seen to include some entries, such as debt retirement, whose origin lay in the capital budget. From the operating budget we developed the cash-flow schedule. Later, this was used to establish an end-of-period

PROJECTED TREASURER'S REPORT

Estimated Position as of December 31, 1962
Prepared September 11, 1962

PART I - Church Benevolences and Operations

Actual Cash on hand, January 1, 1962	$ 3,275
Estimated Receipts during 1962	58,500
Total Available	61,775
Estimated Disbursements during 1962	58,300
Estimated Cash on hand, December 31, 1962	$ 3,475

SOURCES OF RECEIPTS:

Pledges from individuals		$ 48,400
Plate Offering - Church Services		2,800
Plate Offering - Church School		1,000
For use of Neighborhood House	$1,235	
From friends	1,265	2,500
Special Contributions:		
One Great Hour of Sharing	$ 850	
Share Our Surplus	760	
The Rockport Fund (for debt retirement)	500	
Endowment Fund (for debt retirement)	500	2,610
Other receipts		1,190
Estimated Total receipts during 1962		$ 58,500

OBJECT OF DISBURSEMENTS:

Benevolences:		
Middle Atlantic Conference:		
Our Christian World Mission	$6,150	
One Great Hour of Sharing	850	
Share Our Surplus	800	$ 7,800
Other:		
United Church of Christ Home	$ 425	
Washington Assn., United Churches of Christ	275	
Middle Atlantic Conference	240	
Congregational Christian Historical Society	10	
Council of Churches, National Capital Area	300	
Virginia Council of Churches	110	
National Council of Churches	30	
World Council of Churches	30	
Family Service Society	125	
Other	100	1,645
Sub-Total		9,445
Worship and Pastoral Leadership:		
Minister's Salary	$6,300	
Minister's Annuity	705	
Minister's Car Allowance	800	
Minister's Hospitality Allowance	100	
Minister's Utilities	700	8,605
Assistant Minister's Salary	2,800	
Assistant Minister's Annuity	280	
Assistant Minister's Car Allowance	210	
Assistant Minister's Utilities	120	3,410
Pulpit supply		75
Organist and Choir Director		2,100
Music		400
Deacon's Activities		1,110
Social Action Committee		50
Notices and Bulletins		1,800
Sub-Total		17,540

Exhibit 22. Example of *Pro-Forma* Treasurer's Report

Youth Work:
  Associate in Christian Education - salary   3,900
                                - car allowance   225
                                - tuition allowance   <u>75</u>   4,200
  Church school materials   940
  Other Christian Education activities   <u>200</u>
            Sub-Total   5,340

Office Operation:
  Church secretary (salary)   3,300
  Office expenses   820
  Telephone service   760
  Social security taxes   <u>380</u>
            Sub-Total   5,260

Property:
  Custodian (salary)   3,300
  Repairs and maintenance   1,700
  Utilities   3,060
  Insurance   946
  Alterations and equipment   <u>90</u>
            Sub-Total   9,096

Debt Service:
  Interest - Perpetual Building Association   2,290
          - Unsecured Notes   <u>870</u>   3,160
  Debt Retirement - Perpetual Building Association   5,012
                  - Board of Home Missions   1,585
                  - Unsecured Notes   <u>1,862</u>   <u>8,459</u>
            Sub-Total   11,619
      Estimated total disbursements during 1962   <u>$ 58,300</u>

PART II - Pro-forma Balance Sheet, as of December 31, 1962

ASSETS:

  Cash on hand $ 3,475
  Land   10,130
  Buildings   321,250
  Equipment   <u>12,563</u>
     Total Assets   <u>$ 347,418</u>

LIABILITIES:

  Mortgage notes   57,202
  Unsecured notes   13,500
  Mortgage Grants   <u>15,150</u>
     Total Indebtedness $ 85,852

NET WORTH

                                        261,566
     Total Liabilities and Net Worth   <u>$ 347,418</u>

Exhibit 22.   Continued

position, recorded for planning purposes as a *pro forma* treasurer's report.

Most important, we considered a special version of the operating budget, called the appeal budget, designed for distribution to the general membership and the interested public.

In the next chapter, we shall take up the remaining function of the budget in church life and management. This is the function of budgetary control. We shall be concerned with questions such as: "What recording and reporting should occur as part of the budget implementation process?" "How often and in what detail should planned use of resources be checked against actual use?" "What should be done about variance?" "How can the budget react to unforeseen events and contingencies?"

Part III

The Church Budget
in Use

Chapter 8

BUDGETARY CONTROL

MORE THAN IN any other endeavor, we should be concerned in church finance with the problem of laxness in the control of expenditures. Waste should not be tolerated. In business, waste eats into profit. In Government, waste increases national debt and the tax burden. Waste means that resources devoted by their givers to the work of the church have resulted in some of that work going undone. As Methodist Bishop John Wesley Lord has said, "In the economy of God there is no provision for wastefulness." This in itself justifies the detailed attention we have given to church financial management and in particular to programming and budgeting.

The danger of waste due to laxness in expenditures can be overcome if two prerequisites of control of spending are established. First, there must be an arrangement and grouping of items that sets forth all expenses in their proper relationship and necessary detail. Secondly, there must be an inescapable placement of responsibility for each of these expenses upon a specific individual or an organizational element. Individual responsibility is preferred to organizational responsibility.

REPORTING ACCOMPLISHMENTS AND PROBLEMS

Control of expenditures requires a system of recording and reporting the accomplishment of the program and budget, and the problems encountered. This should be established on a periodic basis, usually monthly. The reports should lend themselves to comparison of actual performance against budgeted performance. This requires that the budget be broken down into increments against which the accomplishments and expenses of each successive month may be compared. The cash-flow schedule (Exhibit 21, page 142) serves this purpose very well, but, in the absence of a cash-flow schedule, monthly expenses may be compared against one-twelfth the annual total. The latter, a loose and inefficient approach, is not recommended.

In addition to the month-to-month comparison, there should be a comparison of budget to date with accomplishments to date. As the year progresses, the "to date" column accumulates until finally, at the end of the year, the total budget is accounted for. Exhibit 23, on page 155, shows a format for periodic reporting of actual expenses experienced against amounts budgeted.

IDENTIFYING AND ANALYZING VARIANCE

The mechanics of reporting accomplishment against the budget may be done by the church treasurer assisted by a member of the church office. The analysis of the report is a task for the board of finance. Each significant variation between budgeted and actual amounts must be questioned when it first appears. Variances should not be allowed to run over many months and accumulate significant differences before they are investigated. A member of the board of finance should explore each significant variance with the responsible individual, obtaining a statement as to the reasons underlying the over- or under-expenditure.

The board of finance should not sit in judgment and criticize failure to comply with the budget. Rather, the board of finance should report periodically to the higher boards and committees of the church, and to the pastor, the variances

TREASURER'S REPORT--STATUS OF CHURCH BENEVOLENCE AND OPERATIONS BUDGET

AS OF NOVEMBER 30, 1962

	Budget for Year	Month of November	Year to Date	Balance Remaining for 1 mo.
RECEIPTS:				
Individual Pledges	$ 48,450	$ 4,498	$ 42,144	$ 6,306
Plate Offerings	3,750	420	3,417	333
Use of Neighborhood House	2,900	89	2,129	771
Other	2,500	557	2,148	352
TOTAL RECEIPTS	57,600	5,564	49,838	7,762
EXPENDITURES:				
Benevolences:				
Our Christian World Mission	7,800	1,000	5,847	1,953
Other	1,600	0	1,272	328
Sub-Totals	9,400	1,000	7,119	2,281
Worship and Pastoral Leadership:				
Minister	8,555	635	7,941	614
Assistant Minister	3,450	430	2,952	498
Pulpit Supply	75	0	75	0
Organist & Choir Director	2,160	132	1,921	239
Board of Music	410	70	397	13
Board of Deacons	1,350	52	1,163	187
Social Action Committee	50	1	43	7
Bulletin	1,750	195	1,548	202
Sub-Totals	17,800	1,515	16,040	1,760
Youth Work:				
Assoc. Christian Education	4,210	353	3,857	353
Church School Materials	1,150	5	806	344
Other Christian Education Activities	300	7	142	158
Sub-Totals	5,660	365	4,805	855
Office Operation:				
Church Secretary	3,380	268	3,065	315
Office Expenses	800	97	735	65
Telephone	750	115	703	47
Social Security Taxes	415	0	292	123
Sub-Totals	5,345	480	4,795	550
Property:				
Custodian	3,275	250	2,996	279
Repair & Maintenance	1,600	184	1,540	60
Utilities	3,300	108	2,773	527
Insurance	945	267	948	3
Alterations & Improvements	140	0	81	59
Sub-Totals	9,260	809	8,338	922
Debt Service:				
Interest	3,160	294	2,819	341
Debt Retirement	6,960	341	6,934	26
Sub-Totals	10,120	634	9,753	367
TOTAL EXPENDITURES	$ 57,585	$ 4,804	$ 50,850	$ 6,735
Excess of: Receipts	15	760	–	1,027
Expenditures	–	–	1,012	–

Exhibit 23. Example of Monthly and Year-to-Date Comparison of Actual Expenses Against Amounts Budgeted

that have been identified and the reasons given. Responsibility for corrective action lies with these latter individuals, and involves an understanding and appreciation of the underlying program and the problems encountered therewith.

Not only should the board of finance identify and analyze variances; it should attempt to foresee and forecast financial problems. In this responsibility, use should be made of the *pro forma* financial report and balance sheet previously described (Exhibit 22, page 147). Such forecasts should be looked upon as a service rendered by the board of finance to the operating officials of the church, the latter of whom are concerned primarily with programs being carried out rather than with financial detail.

BUDGET REVISION—THE FLEXIBLE BUDGET CONCEPT

The concept of the flexible budget was mentioned in Chapters 2 and 5. It will be recalled that the flexible budget identified alternative levels of activity that might reasonably be expected to develop during the operating year. Now that reports are actually being received and analyzed, the board of finance may find it necessary to employ this flexible concept and either increase certain elements of the budget or fall back to a lower position. A well-prepared budget will have identified these various possible levels of activity, and also areas of application for funds that might be received in excess of those anticipated, as well as areas of expense that will have to be reduced if receipts do not come up to expectations. Matters such as these, the identification of areas of increased emphasis and areas of possible reduction, should not be postponed until the need for decision arises. They should be done at least tentatively at the time the budget is originally developed and adopted.

Any necessary revision of the budget must be accomplished with full participation of the concerned operating departments. The accusation cannot be allowed to arise that "the board of finance is changing the budget behind our backs." It should never be felt that the budget, once approved and adopted, must stand unchanged. As unforeseen events and contingencies arise, programs and budget entries must be re-examined. The resourceful programs and budget committee, particularly in the larger churches, includes in the budget a "reserve for contingencies." Where this is done the board of finance usually is allowed discretion in applying the reserve to meet unforeseen needs.

SUMMARY OF OUR APPROACH TO CHURCH BUDGET DEVELOPMENT

Budgeting is an administrative process, an integral part of the task of church business management. Budgeting takes its place in a sequence:

First, we plan our goals and objectives.

Second, we program the things we expect to do to gain our objectives, and when we plan to do them.

Then, we budget the costs and the resources.

Planning, programming, and budgeting go on all the time. We are involved in one stage or another the year around. This is not something we do in a few weeks or a month—and then forget for another year.

The program or budget period (the fiscal year) need not be the calendar year. It should begin and end on dates that "make sense" in the life of the individual church.

Budgeting involves individuals from all the various activities of the church. It is not the sole preserve of the treasurer or of the board of finance. Programming and budgeting should be charged to a programs-and-budget committee representing all of the interests of the congregation. Establishment of the procedures to be followed, and the timetable to be observed, are a responsibility of the board of finance.

The details of budgeting, the assembly and analysis of the many items of expense and income, should be done on "worksheets" identifying departmental responsibility and observing accounting conventions. Extensive reports of these details should not be imposed on the general membership. Instead, a separate, attractive, brief program-oriented version of the budget should be prepared and distributed. This is the appeal budget.

Greater attention must be paid to the income portion of the budget. This is a neglected aspect of budgeting in many churches. A thorough analysis of resource potential must precede any fund-raising effort. There should be no reluctance to openly announce the planned sources of church income and the reliance being placed on each.

The budgetary process is not complete until provision is made for control of financial resources during the operating period. This control is based on a schedule of cash-flow, treasurer's periodic reports, and forecasts of financial condition. Good budgets are flexible enough to respond to unanticipated conditions.

Up to this point, we have been concerned primarily with the budgetary process and with the considerations and problems that enter into preparation of the church budget. We have made passing references to the relationship of the budget to other activities of the church, and to the role the budget plays in church life.

In the final chapter, we shall examine church programming and budgeting in a different light, asking such questions as: How can good budgetary procedure enable the church to declare its policies more effectively, define its objectives, and delineate its programs? What constitutes the commitment of a church and its resources to a plan or program? What is the true measure of success in programming and budgeting?

Chapter 9

THE BUDGET IN CHURCH
LIFE AND MANAGEMENT

ON SEVERAL OCCASIONS, the author has heard people say, "I suppose my church has a budget but I have never seen it." Such a remark reflects a deplorable condition. As many people as possible should be brought into the development of the church's program and budget.

Everyone should be conscious of the fact that his church does have a program. All should be aware of the main features of the program, as a reflection of the things the church wishes to do. Every member should feel that he has had an opportunity to express his position regarding the various elements of his church's program. It should not be assumed that all of the works of the church are "good," and that all are therefore uniformly accepted and supported by the membership. Through familiarity with programs as they are developed and proposed, individuals and organized groups of the church develop an interest that is reflected later in greater participation and greater accomplishment. Equally important, individuals and groups recognize that they are developing a statement of needs that ultimately will have to be financed. They are, therefore, prepared and conditioned for announcement of the resources that must be raised during the forthcoming period.

THE BUDGET AS A PROBLEM IDENTIFIER

An observer of governmental activity notes in the fall a flurry of controversy not seen at other times of the year. The reason for this is that the budgets for the following fiscal year are generally presented to the departmental secretaries in September and October. Their presentation recalls to mind, or raises for the first time, many problems that would have remained unnoticed if their financial demands did not raise questions of alternatives.

Not only does the budget identify problems; it also forces decisions on matters that might otherwise go undecided. This can also be illustrated from the realm of governmental budgeting. The President's annual budget message to the Congress, normally delivered early in January, is sent to the printers two to three days before Christmas. Therefore, the observer of the Washington scene will see during mid-December the sudden resolution of many problems, some of which have existed for months, if not years.

Church budgets developed in accordance with good procedures for review of needs and justification of programs also tend to identify problems and to force decisions.

For instance, deficiencies in the condition of property and other facilities are brought to light. Moreover, such deficiencies are stated in concrete terms of dollar requirements. Value judgments have been made at many levels, particularly in regard to discretionary items. What is the relative importance of outfitting the choir with new robes, as opposed to refurnishing and repainting the sanctuary or modernizing the social hall kitchen? As an aid to the making of such judgments, many churches use a program "checklist," an example of which is seen in Exhibit 24, beginning on page 163.

EDUCATION AND YOUTH	NEED FOR IMPROVEMENT				Remarks
	No	Yes	Urgent	Defer	
1. Sunday church school program					
2. Released time school program					
3. Vacation church school program					
4. Day camp program					
5. Adult education program					
6. Training program for teachers who are teaching					
7. Training program for prospective teachers					
8. Full-time Director of Religious Education					
9. Planning for introduction of new LCA Curriculum					
10. Audio-visuals under responsible direction					
11. Subsidies for conventions, schools, retreats					
12. Library facilities for membership					
13. Adult counsellors for youth activities					
14. Promoting church colleges and church vocations to youth					
15. Promote reading of "The Lutheran" and synod publications					
16. Functioning Christian Education Committee meets regularly					
17.					
18.					
PLANT AND PROPERTY					
1. Outside cleanliness of building(s)					
2. Inside cleanliness of building(s)					
3. Furnishings adequate and in good repair					
4. Heating, ventilation, lighting					
4. Floors, stairs and carpeting					
6. Bulletin boards and signs					
7. Landscaping and sidewalks					
8. Janitorial service					
9. Organ and pianos					
10. Rest rooms light, airy and clean					
11. Janitorial equipment and supplies					
12. Annual review of insurance: Fire, Contents, Liability, etc.					
13. Property reappraised within last 3 years					
14. Regular inspection of total plant and equipment					
15. Functioning Church Property Committee meets regularly					
16.					
17.					
18.					

Exhibit 24. Example of a Program Check-List

(Furnished by the Commission on Stewardship, The Lutheran Church in America.)

SOCIAL MINISTRY	NEED FOR IMPROVEMENT				Remarks
	No	Yes	Urgent	Defer	
1. Congregational program of Christian service					
2. Service to emotionally disturbed (in community)					
3. Service to those with financial needs					
4. Services to physically handicapped (blind, deaf, etc.)					
5. Laity trained to visit and aid the sick, shut-ins, and aged					
6. Special transportation assistance					
7. Laity serving as volunteers in local institutions					
8. LWA clothing appeals sponsored twice annually					
9. Sponsor children's and youth activities (besides L.L., Education)					
10. Interpret social problems					
11. Applying ministry of laity in daily life					
12. Homemaker service					
13. Exercise leadership in studying, preventing and correcting social ills					
14. Cooperate in Lutheran Welfare, or other welfare agency efforts					
15. Hospitality to international students					
16. Functioning Social Ministry Committee meets regularly					
17.					
18.					

STEWARDSHIP AND BENEVOLENCE					
1. Stewardship education a year-round concern					
2. Stewardship is understood to be total life commitment					
3. Effective use is made of members' time and abilities					
4. Children's pledges encouraged and offering envelopes used					
5. Tithing and/or proportionate giving emphasized					
6. The offering is related to the worship experience					
7. Budget proposals related to congregation's real ability					
8. Conduct annual every member visit in homes					
9. Formal budget adopted on basis of EMV pledge results					
10. Youth are used in all phases of EMV program					
11. Lutheran Church Foundation facilities and aids are used					
12. "Tell-the-People" packet used effectively					
13. Benevolence funds remitted monthly to synod					
14. Our congregation is steadily moving towards 50/50 giving					
15. Leaders receive the "Stewardship Bulletin" from Stewardship Commission					
16. Leadership attends stewardship conference, schools, workshops, etc.					
17. Functioning Stewardship Committee meets regularly					
18.					
19.					

Exhibit 24. Continued

EVANGELISM AND MEMBERSHIP	NEED FOR IMPROVEMENT				Remarks
	No	Yes	Urgent	Defer	
1. Conduct neighborhood surveys every two years					
2. Regular follow-up on prospect list					
3. Regular membership contact program beyond the EMV					
4. Formal program for educating new members					
5. Assimilate all new members into congregational life					
6. Use local news and broadcast media					
7. Promote local broadcasts of PRT Radio and TV programs					
8. Special outreach to church school parents					
9. Use of Contact and Referral Service					
10. Reach new people in community promptly					
11. Make effective use of materials provided by the Church					
12. Maintain contacts with our youth in college and armed services					
13. Encourage periodic congregational fellowship gatherings					
14. Leadership trained in Evangelism					
15. Program for reclaiming inactive and unresponsive membership					
16. Prepare members for witnessing in daily life					
17. Study congregation through new Life Mission					
18. Conduct occasional Evangelism Missions					
19. Functioning Evangelism Committee meets regularly					
20.					

WORSHIP AND MUSIC					
1. Present hours of services meet needs of area					
2. Attendance by family units stressed					
3. Using the Lutheran Service Book and Hymnal					
4. Hymnals in adequate supply					
5. Director of Music					
6. Children to adult choir training program					
7. Church interior conducive to worship					
8. Special provision for hard of hearing					
9. Choir supplies and facilities					
10. Ushers friendly, helpful and attentive					
11. Altar appointments					
12. Building open for daily meditation					
13. Organ and instruments on regular maintenance schedule					
14. Sunday bulletins aid in worship experience					
15. Members cordial to each other and visitors					
16. Religious art and drama appreciation					
17. Functioning Worship and Music Committee meets regularly					
18.					

Exhibit 24. Continued

PARISH ADMINISTRATION	NEED FOR IMPROVEMENT				Remarks
	No	Yes	Urgent	Defer	
1. Staff sufficient for present and expected opportunities					
2. Competent secretarial assistance					
3. Pastor relieved of administrative detail					
4. Organized voluntary service program					
5. Pastor compelled to take time off every week					
6. Pastor compelled to take one month annual vacation					
7. Budget provision made for guest preachers					
8. Pastor provided with adequate utilities and auto allowances					
9. Good working facilities for entire staff					
10. Salaries of entire staff reviewed annually					
11. Equipment on maintenance and replacement schedules					
12. Book allowance for pastor					
13. Staff participates in LCA benefit programs					
14. Pastor has a discretionary fund to help problem cases					
15. Early consideration of LCA model constitution planned					
16. Congregation regularly informed through parish newsletter					
17. Records well maintained and safeguarded					
18. Periodic evaluation of congregation's program and outreach					
19. Council meets monthly on regular meeting night					
20.					

FINANCE					
1. Records carefully kept according to recommended procedures					
2. Detailed written reports furnished monthly to council					
3. Treasurers and financial secretaries records audited regularly					
4. Minimum two persons count offerings at all times					
5. Offerings not counted during worship service					
6. All persons handling congregational finances bonded					
7. Records carefully safeguarded and accessible to authorized persons					
8. Annual budget submitted to and approved by congregation					
9. Proper budget control maintained					
10. Interest costs regularly reviewed					
11. Mortgages regularly reviewed					
12. Taxes current					
13. Benevolence funds remitted to synod treasurer monthly					
14. Treasurer and financial secretary given full assistance					
15. Federal and State laws on taxes and minimum wages observed					
16. Functioning Finance Committee meets regularly					
17.					
18.					

Exhibit 24.   Continued

THE BUDGET AS A WRITTEN AND SUBSCRIBED COMMITMENT TO ACTION

Out of several hundred budgets examined recently by the author, only one carried a signature indicating that it was an approved and subscribed document. In this case, the signature was that of the president of the board of deacons.

Church budgets should be approved and subscribed to with some degree of formality. After all, a budget represents tremendous effort on the part of a great many people, as well as a culmination of much thought and discussion. The budget will serve as a guide and an authorization during the forthcoming period, and it is going to require support and understanding. For this reason, the appeal budget should be disseminated as broadly as possible. Opportunities should be created to have it discussed, and, finally, to have it submitted to the membership for a vote of adoption.

In the author's church, the working budget is reproduced in several copies and held in the church office for those who wish to examine such detail. The appeal budget is furnished, in many copies, to each board and committee chairman and to neighborhood leaders, who, in turn, distribute it to individual members. Small groups discuss and argue the various points as they see fit. Then an announcement is made in the church bulletin that the budget will be voted on by the congregation in a general meeting. When this is done, the budget is recorded by the church clerk as having been approved and accepted both as an indication of the desires of the congregation and as their commitment to its support.

SUCCESSFUL BUDGETING

There is always danger in an administrative process such as budgeting that successful achievement of the process itself will become an objective. It is not unusual to hear a member of a management group, such as a programs-and-budget committee, proudly describe how close his church came to its budget, as if this were a measure of acuteness in forecasting church activity. Of course, there should be an element of pride in a budgeting job well done, but how closely actual operations match budgets is not particularly important. Far more important is the extent to which programs are realized or attained. In the final analysis, the budget is a success only if the maximum is accomplished with the resources at hand.

Successful budgeting adheres to a few basic principles, chief of which is that the budget should be established on the highest possible level of motivation. A budget should set objectives and establish standards of performance that require effort to attain. At the same time, these objectives and standards should not be set so high that the budget becomes a pressure device or, as so often happens, an excuse when programs are not attained. This idea is extremely important. It must be part of the philosophy under which the church proceeds.

The budget must be firmly anchored in a foundation of planning and programming. There can be no budget of any real value or effectiveness unless it grows out of carefully developed plans and programs.

The meaning of budgetary control must also be clearly established. When properly conceived, this means at least two things. First, the responsible committee or organization head has control over what goes into his budget, reflecting his understanding of the job to be done and the needs of his activity. Second, he will have responsibility for accomplishment of the program, and as part of this responsibility he must come forward when events occur that affect his program and the financial needs related thereto.

Successful budgeting requires a clear organizational relationship. Many failures in budgeting have been laid at the door of the budgetary procedure when they should have been blamed on poor organization. Each organizational element should have a clear concept of where its responsibilities begin and end. Each must have a responsible head to whom appropriate church officers have given authority commensurate with his responsibilities. Each such responsible head must have a clear understanding as to whom he reports to in the local church hierarchy.

Programming and budgeting cannot be satisfactorily performed unless it is supported by a sound accounting system. The accounting system must be complete and at the same time relatively simple. More important, it must be one that provides for the reflection of operating facts, as well as the figures necessary to meet accounting conventions. Church accounting is approached in many ways, and many technicalities must be mastered if it is to be effective in relation to church budgeting. Many aspects of this subject are presented in another book in this series, *Church Accounting Methods,* by Arthur L. Walker.

The programming and budgeting process must have broad participation. This must begin at the top with the higher church officers and committees, both ordained and lay. Their participation should set an example for others throughout the organization. Programs will not succeed without widespread participation and support.

Lastly, it must be remembered that the church programs-and-budget committee, the church board of finance, the treasurer, and the financial secretary must all maintain the correct attitude toward their budgetary responsibilities. Their job is to establish, maintain, and coordinate a system of programming and budgeting and to assure the annual development of a sound and representative program budget. Their job continues into the operating phase, since the budget is used in management of church business affairs and in appraisal of accomplishment. All of this must be done by working with and through the responsible individuals through-out the church. The boards and individuals just named should not force themselves or their requirements upon others. They should perform a supporting role, allowing the programming and operating decisions to be made by those of their associates who have direct responsibility.

HUMAN ASPECTS

As we see in so many fields of endeavor, human aspects of a matter often overshadow the technical aspects. Churches as well as other groups have much to learn, and to exemplify, in the matter of overcoming human problems of budgeting. Churchmen find it difficult to establish a budgetary pro-cedure, where one has not existed, because of three things:

> The education of most church members has not included an orientation to the concept of budgeting; therefore, budgeting is not generally understood.
>
> It is difficult to stimulate interest in any kind of budget.
>
> There seems to be an inherent mistrust of budgets.

These attitudes are based on experiences that have oc-curred all too often. Budgets have been used as pressure devices, resulting in increased tension, aggressive attitudes, and loss of effectiveness. Accounting and budgeting staffs have attempted to add to their own feeling of success and importance by using the budget as a method of finding fault and pointing out failures in others. In too many cases, budget discussions have highlighted only faults and deficiencies and all too seldom have called attention to successful perform-ance. As part of this same criticism, all too often reports based on the budget reflect only results, with no indication of the reasons behind the results. Therefore, we might high-light the troubles of a department without explaining the reasons behind them. Overcoming these human reactions is a challenge to be met by broad participation and successful communications between those responsible for assembling the program and budget and the operating individuals affected by it. This is not an area in which great gains can be made through haste. Patience must be exercised in establishing or revising programming and budgeting procedures.

BUDGETING TIME AND TALENT

The imaginative church will take advantage of the interest generated in programs and the budget to extend their procedures to include the budgeting of personal time and talents.

We have used the term "resource planning." Time and talent are resources of greater importance than dollars. As each of the programs of the church is studied and discussed, the record established should show not only the dollars needed, but personnel resources as well. Later, when membership is being canvassed, a pledge of time and talent is also asked. The *Church Program and Budgets Builder,* a publication of the United Church of Christ, recommends a form for such a pledge. It is included as Exhibit 25, on page 172.

BUDGETING DON'TS

Working with budget officers throughout industry, the Financial Executives Institute (formerly known as Controllers Institute of America) has prepared a "don't" list that deserves careful study. As reproduced below, the language has been modified slightly to make it appropriate to our purpose. The *don'ts* are:

Don't install a budget system until leaders are willing to accept or comply with full cooperation.

Don't divide responsibility below the level of policy and program determination.

PROPOSED PERSONNEL BUDGET

Statement of Time and Talent Needs

Church...Place...

MY COMMITMENT OF TIME AND TALENT

Name.. Address...

This *PROPOSED PERSONNEL BUDGET* with *My Commitment of Time and Talent* is an opportunity list for your use. Our Committee hopes that you will check many points where you intend to enlist — or re-enlist — in the church's work for 19........ Please check the column beside the opportunities for service you are interested in and discuss them further if you wish with the Visitors who will call upon you Sunday, ... After re-checking this list with the Visitors you may sign it as your intended contribution of time and talent to the better work of our church this coming year.

....**Chairman,**
Program and Budgets Committee

AREA AND TYPE OF SERVICE

PUBLIC WORSHIP

	Persons Needed	My Pledge (check)
Present average Sunday attendance, ...; for next year		
New voices for the choir:		
Sopranos		
Altos		
Tenors		
Basses		
A corps of ushers, rotating every two weeks		
Transportation for those otherwise unable to attend church.		
Drivers with cars —		

Note:
The above entries are given only to suggest the form which this Budget may take. Each church will determine its own needs and list them under the following heads:

	Persons Needed	My Pledge (check)
PUBLIC WORSHIP		
PERSONAL DEVOTIONS AND DISCIPLINE		
EVANGELISM		
STEWARDSHIP		
SOCIAL ACTION		
CHRISTIAN EDUCATION:		
General		
Children		
Youth		
Adults		
MISSIONARY EDUCATION		
ADULT FELLOWSHIP GROUPS		
THE MINISTRY		
ADMINISTRATION		
GOD'S HOUSE AND ITS CARE		

*These are the same headings as used in the section of this Builder, entitled "Building the Program."

Exhibit 25. Sample Form for a Pledge of Time and Talent

(Furnished by the Stewardship Council, United Church of Christ.)

Don't let the budget be a creation of the programs-and-budget committee alone. It is essentially an operational function of department heads. The committee is the coordinator and adviser. Explanation of variances from the budget is the responsibility of department heads.

Don't place budget authority in the hands of anyone with partisan influences.

Don't force budgets on departmental heads. Make the budget a joint venture. Work out the results together.

Don't present a master budget plan without consulting all parties concerned.

Don't classify all expenditures on the same basis. Consider as "Urgent," "Current," or "Desirable" projects.

Don't fail to have a definite plan for administration of the budget after it has been established.

Don't overlook the unique opportunity afforded to the programs-and-budget committee to act as a liaison between the various operating and staff departments.

Don't permit anyone on the programs-and-budget committee to have an indifferent attitude toward budgeting. An enthusiastic attitude is a requisite of a successful budget.

Don't fail to keep and circulate an up-to-date budget procedure. Refer to it frequently.

Don't fail to praise individuals who are responsible for good planning and performance, and don't fail to assist those whose planning is below par.

Don't depend entirely on a tailor-made budget from a publication. A general outline of a budget may be available, but usually this form will require adaptation to your specific requirements.

BUDGETING AND THE RELIGIOUS TASK

Rabbi Jacob D. Schwarz, Director Emeritus of Synagogue Activities for The Union of American Hebrew Congregations, has written: "Financial planning is indispensable. Haphazard financing with uncertain income at one end and unregulated expenditures at the other should be replaced by well-defined planning, calling for the expenditure of definite sums of money which will present a direct challenge to adequate support by the membership." In this book, we have shown how such financial planning can be approached and accomplished. But we cannot be satisfied with our current methods. Our methods of church business management must improve with the times. We must examine every opportunity and innovation, asking the question, "Does this present a better way to perform God's work?"

We began this book with the comment that every church or synagogue is a spiritual group, a social group, and an economic unit. Most of our consideration here has been for the church as an economic unit. It is important that we close with a return to the basic truth that the church is a religious institution.

The accusation is often made that churches have become business or semibusiness activities, and that we have become so caught up in the successful running of the church that it is common for many to think that these activities are identical with religion. This problem has been studied by the Reverend John Heuss, of New York City's Trinity Parish, who, after discussing the series of promotional, organizational, and semicommercial activities of the church, observes that answers must be found to several questions, the first two of which are: "What is the true religious work of this parish?" and "How can all that is done in this parish set that true religious task forward?"

Let us pray that the program we develop, and the budget by which the resources are marshaled to accomplish that program, reflect in every way the true religious work of the parish, and that our efforts in the field of church budget development may contribute to successful accomplishment of the religious task before us.

Appendices

OUTLINE FOR CONDUCTING DISCUSSION GROUPS ON CHURCH BUDGET DEVELOPMENT

Basic and General Considerations in Budget Development

  I. Basic considerations
    A. Purposes of budgeting
    B. Advantages and limitations of budgeting
    C. Essentials for effective budgeting
    D. Programming and budgeting terminology
    E. Length and terminal dates of budget period
    F. Budget approval procedure
    G. Budgetary control
  II. Introduction to the operating budget
    A. Expenditure planning
    B. Income planning
  III. The capital budget
  IV. Financial planning
    A. Cash-flow schedules
    B. *Pro forma* statements and financial reports

Identifying and Analyzing the Financial Needs of the Church

  I. Study of significant areas of need
    A. Pastoral leadership and related expenses
    B. Administration and staff remuneration
    C. Religious education
    D. Benevolences and charities
    E. Apportionments and assessments
    F. Property maintenance

    G. Promotional activities
    H. Debt retirement
  II. Study of the operating period
    A. Expenses underestimated
    B. Expenses overestimated

Identifying and Analyzing the Financial Resources of the Church

    I. Study of significant sources of church income
      A. Pledges
      B. Plate offerings
      C. Gifts
      D. Income from use of facilities
      E. Special events
      F. Endowments and investments
      G. Legacies
   II. Study of the operating period
      A. Income underestimated
      B. Income overestimated

Sequence and Timing in Development of the Church Budget

    I. Sequence of principal actions
      A. Assembling and reviewing the programs and plans of all activities of the church
      B. Studying the financial needs of the church
      C. Studying the current and projected income of the church
      D. Preparing the appeal version of the budget
      E. Conducting the post-canvass review and reappraisal
      F. Obtaining approval of the membership
      G. Establishing and exercising budgetary control
   II. The budget preparation and implementation calendar
      A. Establishing the fiscal period
      B. Determining the budget timetable

Preparing and Administering the Budget

    I. Preparing the operating budget working papers
      A. Format and titling

B. Identifying planned income
C. Identifying planned expense
II. Preparing the appeal budget
III. Preparing the capital budget
IV. Preparing the financial plan
  A. The cash-flow schedule
  B. *Pro forma* statements and reports
V. Administering the budget
  A. Reporting accomplishments and problems
  B. Meeting contingencies

SOURCE MATERIALS FOR THE DISCUSSION LEADER

Chapters or sections on planning, programming, and budgeting will be found in the following sources.

Popular books used in basic college courses in management, and in industry, and government-sponsored executive development programs:

Jucius, Michael J., and William E. Schlender. *Elements of Managerial Action*. Homewood, Ill.: Richard D. Irwin, Inc., 1960.

Koontz, Harold, and Cyril O'Donnell. *Principles of Management*. New York: McGraw-Hill Book Co., 1964.

McFarland, Dalton E. *Management Principles and Practices*. New York: Macmillan Co., 1958.

Newman, William H. *Administrative Action*. Englewood Cliffs, N.J.: Prentice-Hall, Inc., 1951.

Terry, George R. *Principles of Management*. Homewood, Ill.: Richard D. Irwin, Inc., 1960.

More recent and more advanced books:

Albers, Henry H. *Organized Executive Action*. New York: John Wiley & Sons, Inc., 1961.

Bellows, Roger, Thomas Q. Gilson, and George S. Odiorne. *Executive Skills*. Englewood Cliffs, N.J.: Prentice-Hall, Inc., 1962.

NEWMAN, WILLIAM H., and CHARLES E. SUMMER, JR. *The Process of Management.* Englewood Cliffs, N.J.: Prentice-Hall, Inc., 1961.

Books dealing directly with church business management.

BRAMER, JOHN C. *Efficient Church Business Management.* Philadelphia: Westminster Press, 1960.

HOLT, DAVID R. *Handbook of Church Finance.* New York: Macmillan Co., 1960.

JOHNSON, F. ERNEST, and J. EMORY ACKERMAN. *The Church as Employer, Money Raiser, and Investor.* New York: Harper & Bros., 1959.

LEACH, WILLIAM H. *Handbook of Church Management.* Englewood Cliffs, N.J.: Prentice-Hall, Inc., 1958.

NATIONAL ASSOCIATION OF CHURCH BUSINESS ADMINISTRATORS. *Proceedings of the Fourth Annual Conference of July 19-22, 1960.* Columbus, Ohio: North Broadway Methodist Church.

WALKER, ARTHUR L. *Church Accounting Methods,* Englewood Cliffs, N.J.: Prentice-Hall, Inc., 1964.

Periodicals:

Church Administration. Monthly. The Sunday School Board, Southern Baptist Convention, 127 Ninth Avenue, North, Nashville 3, Tennessee.

Church Management. Monthly. Church Management, Inc., 2491 Lee Boulevard, Cleveland Heights 18, Ohio.

Proceedings of Workshop Conference. Biennially. National Association of Temple Administrators, 838 Fifth Avenue, New York 21, N.Y.

GLOSSARY OF PROGRAMMING AND
BUDGETING TERMINOLOGY

appeal budget—A version of the church operating budget prepared for general dissemination. Provides summary financial
information and stresses major activities and programs, and
planned sources of income.

board—A permanent, or standing, organization legally created
by the constitution of the church. Membership normally
elected. Has continuing responsibility.

budget—A dollar expression of plans and programs prepared as
a series of documents reflecting anticipated resources and
expenses, and their timing.

budgetary—Pertaining to the budget, as, "the budgetary process."

budgeting—The act of preparing the budget.

capital budget—The portion or element of the budget pertaining
to acquisition of capital assets: land, buildings, equipment.

cash-flow schedule—The portion or element of the budget in
which annual totals are subdivided into monthly (or weekly)
amounts for more detailed management. Also called the
financial plan.

committee—A working group appointed to perform a specific
task. Representative of all interested elements. Normally disbanded upon completion of the task.

control—Measurement of progress against objectives. The evaluation of accomplishments as compared to what was planned, programmed, and budgeted. Overcoming deficiencies or discrepancies through corrective action.

fiscal year—The period of time encompassed by the program and budget. Normally of 12 months duration, but may begin on any chosen date.

forecast—A deliberate and systematic estimate of what the future holds; our best judgment of what will happen unless we plan otherwise.

obligate—To bind the church to an item of expense, such as to sign a purchase order or hire an employee.

operating budget—The budget for current expenses and benevolences of the church. Contrast to capital budget.

operating period—The current period. The fiscal year in which we are now acting, carrying out the plans, programs, and budget previously made.

organizational (departmental) *budgeting*—A form of budgeting under which each of the several organizations within the church make its own program and budget decisions and manages its own finances. Contrast to unified budgeting.

plan—A deliberately determined course of future action, consistent with policy and objectives and taking into account conditions known or assumed to exist.

planning period—The first of the three periods: planning period, programming period, budget period. The years furthest in the future, beyond those we are now programming and budgeting.

policy—A predetermined approach to a problem or situation that can be expected to occur; an attitude determined beforehand.

program—The detail for accomplishment of a plan; the time and money involved; the specific actions to be taken.

programming period—The intermediate of the three periods: planning period, programming period, budget period. The fiscal year after the year being budgeted.

unified budgeting—A form of budgeting under which the total resources and total needs of the church are treated as a unit. Program and budget decision-making is church-wide. The church is unified in its fund raising. Contrast to organizational budgeting.

DUTIES OF BOARDS, COMMITTEES, AND INDIVIDUALS

The following descriptions of duties of various boards, committees, and individuals are offered as a general guide for the placement of responsibility among those concerned with church finance. Individual church practices and designations will vary considerably.

This appendix is consistent with the body of this book in that it describes a programs-and-budget committee constituted separately from the board of finance. This is done because of the values seen in program and budget decision-making by a group more representative of the entire life of the church than is the average board of finance. Many churches will see fit to combine the duties of these two groups. In doing so, they should recognize that they sacrifice the objectivity of a separate committee. They also reduce the number of individuals given an opportunity to involve themselves in this aspect of the work of the church.

DUTIES OF THE BOARD OF FINANCE

The board of finance shall:

Oversee the financial affairs of the church and its several departments specifically—

185

Supervise and approve the collection and expenditure of all church funds. (Authority may be delegated to approve expenditures made in accordance with the budget.)

Approve the procedures and systems of accounts used by the treasurer and the financial secretary.

Establish procedures for handling offerings, including counting methods and the establishment of a roster of counters.

Insure proper safeguards for all church moneys.

Confer with personnel of operating activities on problems of finance.

Report periodically to the board of deacons, the church council, or other higher authority as required.

Establish procedures for and conduct canvasses for pledge and dues submissions.

Establish procedures for the annual development of the church program and budget.

Promulgate the financial policy of the church as handed down by the board of deacons, the church council, the pastor, and others in policy-making positions.

Establish the timetable of program and budget development and implementation.

Periodically report on the status of accomplishment of the program and budget.

Develop and recommend ways of meeting unforeseen financial needs.

DUTIES OF THE PROGRAMS-AND-BUDGET COMMITTEE

The programs-and-budget committee shall:

Lead the congregation in identifying the purposes and objectives of the church.

Evaluate and coordinate the program proposals of the several departments or organizations.

Determine the potential of the congregation—its resources in terms of time, talent, and money.

Plan the budget, adjusting and replanning as the cycle progresses.

Present the program and budget to the congregation for consideration, discussion, and approval.

Establish a record of their work and deliberations, to be passed to the committee of the following year.

DUTIES OF THE TREASURER

Under the supervision of the board of finance, the treasurer shall:

Receive, record, and deposit all moneys of the church.

Expend church moneys in accordance with the authority delegated.

Render a monthly report of the status of the treasury and of expenditures against the budget; report financial problems and major developments as they occur.

Arrange a periodic (normally annual) audit of church financial records.

Arrange bonding for himself and others as necessary.

Provide, on request, historical data concerning past expenditures for use by the programs-and-budget committee.

DUTIES OF THE FINANCIAL SECRETARY

Under the supervision of the board of finance, the financial secretary shall:

Maintain a record of all remitted pledges, contributions and offerings, including a separate account in the name of each contributor.

Furnish numbered and dated pledge envelopes to all pledging members who desire them.

Render quarterly and annual statements to all contributors of record.

Provide, on request, historical data concerning past giving for use by the programs-and-budget committee.

DUTIES OF THE BUSINESS MANAGER (ADMINISTRATOR)

The business manager, or administrator, shall:

Implement administrative decisions of the boards, commissions, and committees; specifically—

Supervise the business and fiscal operations of the church.

Instruct and supervise the office and custodial staff.

Administer salaries and wages, insurance, and tax matters.

Purchase goods and services.

Supervise and safeguard the physical property of the church.

Serve as a source of church business information to the congregation and the public.

Coordinate the scheduling of church activities and the use of church facilities, maintaining a master calendar; and edit and publish a church bulletin.

INDEX